MUNICIPAL CIVIL SERVICE COMMISSION

OF

THE CITY OF NEW YORK

RULES AND CLASSIFICATION

As Prescribed and Established December 4, 1903

With Amendments to July 11, 1914

THE GENERAL REGULATIONS OF THE COMMISSION
THE CIVIL SERVICE LAW

COMMISSIONERS:

HENRY MOSKOWITZ, President

DARWIN R. JAMES, Jr. ALEXANDER KEOGH

ROBT. W. BELCHER, Secretary

JOHN F. SKELLY, Assistant Secretary

MAIN OFFICE:

MUNICIPAL BUILDING

ARTES
SCIENTIA
VERITAS
LIBRARY OF THE
UNIVERSITY OF MICHIGAN
TUEBOR
CIRCUMSPICE

MUNICIPAL

CIVIL SERVICE COMMISSION

OF

THE CITY OF NEW YORK

RULES AND CLASSIFICATION

As Prescribed and Established December 4, 1903

With Amendments to July 11, 1914

THE GENERAL REGULATIONS OF THE COMMISSION
THE CIVIL SERVICE LAW

COMMISSIONERS:

HENRY MOSKOWITZ, President

DARWIN R. JAMES, Jr. ALEXANDER KEOGH

ROBT. W. BELCHER, Secretary

JOHN F. SKELLY, Assistant Secretary

THE TROW PRESS, NEW YORK

4116-14-3500 (T)

MUNICIPAL CIVIL SERVICE RULES

CONTENTS

MUNICIPAL CIVIL SERVICE RULES

OF

THE CITY OF NEW YORK

Rule I.

DEFINITION OF TERMS.

The several terms, hereinafter mentioned, whenever used in these rules or in any regulations in force thereunder, shall be construed as follows:

1. The "Civil Service of The City of New York," which may be designated for convenient reference the "City Service," includes all offices and positions of trust or employment in the service of the city, of whatever function, designation or compensation.

2. The term "Classified Service" refers to that portion of the City Service that is arranged in classes under these rules, for the purposes of the Civil Service Law, and includes all of such offices and positions except elective officers; the officers and employees of the Board of Aldermen; election boards or officers appointed under section 6 of article II of the Constitution; the head or heads of any department of the city government; and persons employed as superintendents, principals or teachers in the public schools.

3. The term "Class" refers to the Exempt Class, the Competitive Class, the Non-Competitive Class, or the Labor Class, as defined in The Civil Service Law.

4. The term "Grade" refers to subdivisions of the Competitive Class arranged for purposes of promotion, and based upon the relative character of the duties, or upon the amount of compensation, regularly attaching to the positions contained therein.

5. The term "Classification" refers to the arrangement, in schedule form, of the titles, offices and positions in the several classes

and grades, which is appended hereto, and which forms an integral part of these rules.

6. The term "Commission," when used by itself, refers to the Municipal Civil Service Commission.

7. The term "Appointing Officer" refers to the officer, commission, board or body having the power of appointment to subordinate offices or positions in any municipal department, office, board, court or institution.

8. The term "Veteran," when used by itself, refers to honorably discharged soldiers, sailors or marines of the Army or Navy of the United States in the late Civil War, who are citizens and residents of this State.

9. The term "Laborer" refers to any mechanic, skilled or unskilled laborer employed, or seeking employment, in a position in the Labor Class.

10. The term "Position," when used by itself, refers to any classified office, position or employment.

11. The term "Compensation" refers to the annual salary attaching to an office or position, or to its equivalent if stated by the day, week or month, and shall include proper commutation for lodging or board when either is furnished at the expense of the City, such rate of commutation to be fixed by regulation of the Commission.

12. The masculine pronoun "he" and its derivatives, wherever employed, includes the feminine pronoun "she" and its derivatives.

13. The term "day" or "days," wherever employed, refers to days on which the city departments are open for the transaction of public business.

Rule II.

GENERAL PROVISIONS.

1. All appointments, promotions, transfers, reinstatements or selections for employment in the Classified Service shall be made according to the merit and fitness of candidates therefor, and in the manner prescribed by these rules.

2. No appointing officer shall appoint, promote or employ any subordinate officer or employee in the Classified Service, or in any way change the official status of any such officer or employee, except in accordance with these rules, and no such appointment, pro-

motion, employment or change of status made in contravention of any provision of these rules shall be valid.

3. No appointment to or selection for, or removal from any office, position or employment in the Classified Service, and no change in the official status of any person in such service shall be in any manner affected or influenced by the political opinions or affiliations of any applicant, or of any officer or employee. No inquiry made by or on behalf of any nominating or appointing officer, nor any question in any form of application or in any examination, shall be framed so as to elicit, and no answer shall be given so as to disclose, any information whatsoever concerning such opinions or affiliations; and no application or recommendation involving any such disclosure shall be received, filed or considered.

4. No person in the City Service shall use his official authority or influence to coerce the political action of any person or body; and no discrimination shall be exercised, promised or threatened by any such person in favor of or against any applicant, officer or employee in the Classified Service because of his political opinions or affiliations, or because he has declined to contribute to any political fund or to render any political service.

5. No person shall be appointed to or employed in any position in the Classified Service under any title or designation not appropriate to the duties he is regularly to perform, and no person in the said service shall be transferred to or, unless under express authority of law, assigned to perform the duties of, any position subject to competitive examination, except in accordance with Rule XIV. or with Clause 13 of Rule XIX.

6. The violation by any person in the City Service of any provision of the Civil Service Law or of these rules, shall be considered sufficient cause for the removal of such person.

Rule III.

ORGANIZATION AND POWERS OF THE COMMISSION.

1. The Municipal Civil Service Commission shall have authority to prescribe such regulations for the instruction of its officers and for the execution of these rules as may not be inconsistent therewith, and wherever practicable, shall prescribe blank forms for all applications, certificates, reports, records and returns required

thereunder. The Commission shall have authority to examine at any time, either directly or through its Secretary, or Examiners, such books, records or papers, filed in any city department or office as have any bearing on the operation of the Civil Service Law or of these rules, and may, in the course of any investigation it may make under the authority conferred by the City Charter, require the production of such books, records or papers, or the attendance of officers or employees as witnesses, at its own office, or other place of meeting. The failure of any person in the City Service to produce with reasonable promptness such books, papers or records, or to give testimony in any such investigation, when called upon to do so, shall be considered sufficient cause for the removal of such person.

2. The Commission shall choose from its own membership a President, who shall serve during its pleasure, and who, subject to the directions of the Commission, shall have such general authority and responsibility in the administration of these rules as shall not be inconsistent with the powers reserved to the Commission by the Civil Service Law or by these rules, or vested directly in some other officer. The Commission may appoint a Secretary, an Assistant Secretary, a Chief Examiner and such examiners, clerks and others as the efficiency of its work may require.

3. The Secretary, the Chief Examiner, the Assistant Chief Examiners and such other Examiners as may be designated by the Commission, shall constitute an Advisory Board for the discussion of methods of examination and rating and of such other matters as the Commission may refer to them. The Commission may, whenever necessary, secure the assistance of experts in an examination of a special or technical character. An examination of candidates for the position of Civil Service Examiner shall be conducted by the Commission or by experts employed therefor; but no person shall at any time be employed as an Examiner for positions in the Competitive Class who is a public officer, other than a notary public or a commissioner of deeds, or who is employed in any other Department of the City government.

4. In advance of any amendment to these rules, or in advance of any amendment of the Classification by which any position shall be subjected to, or exempted from competitive examination, public notice shall be given by the Commission, through advertisement in the "City Record" for not less than three days, and on the request of any interested party a public hearing shall be allowed.

Rule IV.

CLASSIFICATION.

1. The Classified Service shall be arranged in four general classes which shall be known, respectively, as the ***Exempt***, the ***Competitive***, the *Non-Competitive* and the *Labor Class*.

2. The positions in each of the aforesaid classes shall be those specifically designated, under the head of each, in the appended Classification; except that all positions, whether now existing or hereafter created, of whatever functions, designations or compensation, the titles of which are not so designated, shall be deemed to be in the Competitive Class.

3. The Competitive Class and the Labor Class shall be subdivided, for the purposes of these rules, as hereinafter provided.

Rule V.

THE EXEMPT CLASS.

1. Appointments to positions in the Exempt Class may be made without examination; but the appointing officer shall in each case submit to the Commission, in such form as the Commission shall prescribe, a certificate showing (*a*) the title of the position; (*b*) the full name and residence of the appointee; (*c*) the place of his residence during the five years immediately preceding appointment; (*d*) his previous appointments, and periods of service, if any, in the public service; and (*e*) his qualifications for the office or position to be filled.

The Commission may accept such certificate, if it be in accordance with this rule, as a notice of appointment, to take effect on the date of its receipt.

2. Not more than one appointment shall be made to or under the title of any office or position in the Exempt Class unless a different number is specifically mentioned in the Classification.

Rule VI.

THE COMPETITIVE CLASS.

1. Appointments shall be made to or employment shall be given in positions in the Competitive Class that are not filled through

promotion, transfer, reduction or reinstatement, by selection, in the manner hereinafter provided, from among those persons graded highest on the most nearly appropriate eligible list resulting from open competitive examination; except as provided by Rule XII.

2. For the purposes of such examinations, and of regulated promotion where practicable, the Competitive Class shall be subdivided as follows:

Part I.—All positions, of whatever function, description or compensation, not included in any of the subdivisions following, to be known as "The Ungraded Service."

Part II.—Positions of a clerical nature to be known as "The Clerical Service."

Part III.—Positions requiring knowledge of civil engineering to be known as "The Engineering Service."

Part IV.—Positions as Supervisors of public work and conditions to be known as "The Inspection Service."

Part V.—Positions requiring a knowledge of the law to be known as "The Legal Service."

Part VI.—Positions to be known as "The Attendance Service."

Part VII.—The uniformed forces of the Police Department, excepting Matrons and Surgeons, to be known as "The Police Service."

Part VIII.—The uniformed forces of the Fire Department to be known as "The Fire Service."

Part IX.—The uniformed forces of the Department of Correction to be known as "The Prison Service."

Part X.—The uniformed forces of the Department of Street Cleaning to be known as "The Street Cleaning Service."

Part XI.—Positions in the ferry service of the Department of Docks and Ferries to be known as "The Ferry Service."

Part XII.—Positions requiring a knowledge of medicine to be known as the "Medical Service."

3. The positions in the foregoing Parts, except Part I, shall, for purposes of promotion, be arranged in grades, which, so far as they shall have been established, shall be the grades fixed by law or ordinance, and which shall be as designated in the Classification.

The positions included in each subdivision, and in each grade, shall be those designated under the head of each in the Classification.

4. Whenever it is shown to the satisfaction of the Commission to be practicable, and in the interest of good administration, to grade, for purposes of promotion, positions or groups of positions not previously graded, the Commission shall, by such amendment of the rules as may be necessary, establish a new subdivision, em-

bodying such grades, under such general head as it may deem appropriate.

5. The titles of positions in the Competitive Class as set forth in the Classification are descriptive of the duties and functions attaching generally to such positions, or to groups of positions of similar or corresponding character, and not necessarily to particular positions. The titles appearing on the official roster and on pay-rolls shall, so far as practicable, conform to those of the Classification, and the Commission, to meet this requirement, may at any time authorize a change in a roster title, if such change be consistent with the rules governing transfer or promotion. To define more exactly the duties of particular positions, or to fix such positions in the peculiar organization of a department or office, appropriate sub-titles, or "office titles," may be employed, in the discretion of the head of such department or office or of the Board of Estimate and Apportionment; but such sub-titles need not appear either on the roster or on any pay-roll.

6. Examinations for positions in the Competitive Class shall be held and eligible lists therefor shall be established, only under titles designated in the Classification; except where it is shown that the qualifications required for a particular position are of a peculiar or unusual character, to which no classified title is applicable; the Commission, in such case, may hold a special examination for appointment to such position, but shall state in its minutes and in its annual report the reasons for which each such special examination is held.

Original appointments, in a graded service, shall be made, in each case, to positions of the lowest grade established in the department, office or institution in which such appointments occur; except where it is found to be not practicable to fill a vacancy or vacancies in a higher grade through promotion.

The Commission may hold examinations for designated grades of a position in a graded service to secure eligibles for vacancies therein that it is not practicable to fill through promotion; or for a designated compensation or range of compensation under the title of any position in the ungraded service, or in the engineer service, that it is not practicable to fill by selection from an existing list; but the difference, in such latter case, between the compensation so designated and the compensation attaching to a list already in force, under the same title, shall in no case be less than three hundred dollars.

Rule VII.

COMPETITIVE EXAMINATIONS.

1. The Commission shall hold examinations for appointment to positions in the Competitive Class, and shall fix the dates therefor and the conditions thereof, whenever necessary, to meet or to anticipate the needs of the City Service.

So far as practicable, examinations for admission to positions in a graded service shall be held periodically, and the dates thereof shall be published at the beginning of each year, with such information with reference to the conditions of each as can be given.

2. All such examinations, whether previously scheduled or otherwise, shall be advertised for at least two weeks prior to the final date for the receipt of applications therefor, daily in the "City Record"; and in such other publications and at such times as the Commission may designate for each examination. Such examination shall also be announced at least two weeks prior to the date therefor in notices posted conspicuously in the offices of the Commission, and at such other places as the Commission may deem proper.

In each case such advertisement in the "City Record," or notice so posted, shall set forth (*a*) the title of the position; (*b*) the grade, if in a graded service; (*c*) the time and place of examination; (*d*) the subjects of examination, in detail, with the weight given to each; (*e*) such preliminary or special qualifications as may be required by law or by the appointing officer, with the approval of the Commission, in respect to age, residence, physical fitness, previous experience or training, or other particulars; (*f*) the number of vacancies existing, so far as known, or likely to exist within a year, that will be filled by appointment from the eligible list to be formed; (*g*) the compensation or range of compensation to be paid; (*h*) the date upon which the receipt of applications will close, and (*i*) such other information as the Commission may deem pertinent or necessary.

Such advertisement in other newspapers or periodicals shall, where practicable, set forth the same particulars, and shall at least set forth the title of the position, the time and place of the examination and its subjects, and shall then refer applicants to the "City Record," or to the posted notices, for further details.

3. Every examination, except for the position of Civil Service Examiner, shall be under the responsible direction of the Chief Examiner, who shall consult, when necessary, with appointing

officers concerning the qualifications required for particular positions; but such examinations shall be free from the influence or participation, in any manner, either of the appointing officer or of any person other than the Commission or its designated officers or employees.

4. The subjects of examination and the relative weight given to each, where not fixed by these rules or by regulation, shall be fixed by the Chief Examiner, subject to the direction of the Commission.

The Chief Examiner shall assign the examiners for a given examination, or for a given subject, except where experts are employed, and all written questions prepared by such examiners or experts shall be placed in his custody in advance of such examination. Such questions shall be printed, from type or other process, under his immediate supervision and, unless relieved by the Commission, he shall be responsible for their safe-keeping. So far as practicable, such printing shall be done on the day of examination.

5. The examinations shall be practical in their character and shall relate to such matters as will test fairly and adequately the relative fitness and capacity of the persons to be examined for the discharge of the duties of the service, or of the position, into which they seek to enter. For positions of a designated grade or compensation they shall vary in strictness as the grade or the amount of compensation advances.

6. Whenever, in the judgment of the Commission, physical qualifications are requisite, candidates shall be required to pass a physical examination, and be certified as qualified in such respect, either before admission to examination, or before record on the proper eligible list, or before certification for appointment, as the Commission may announce.

The Commission may further direct oral examinations or special practical tests of fitness.

Where the duties of any classified position are of a character requiring the appointment of persons within particular limitations of age the Commission may, subject to the provisions of the Civil Service Law relating to veterans, fix such limitation by Regulation.

7. In advance of examination for a position the duties of which are scientific, professional or technical, candidates shall be required to present evidences of the special education or preliminary training they have had tending to qualify them for such position; and the

Commission may also, if in its judgment, fitness for such position demands, require, as a condition of examination, evidence of practical experience for a satisfactory term, in such service, profession, art or trade.

Training and experience, of a character tending to show peculiar and espcial fitness for the position examined for, may be rated as a fixed subject of examination, but a candidate in stating such training and experience shall be required to give references through which such statements may be satisfactorily verified.

8. Where the position to be filled involves fiduciary responsibility the appointing officer, where otherwise permitted by law, may require a candidate to furnish a bond or other security as a condition precedent to appointment and shall notify the Commission of the amount and necessary details thereof. The Commission, in such case, shall state in the announcement of the examination, that the candidate must be prepared to furnish such bond or security if called upon to do so.

9. All examinations shall be in writing, except such as relate to physical qualities, and except as herein otherwise provided. Whenever oral questioning is prescribed, as part of any scheme of examination, so far as practicable a stenographic record of such oral questions and of the answers thereto shall be filed with the papers of the candidate. All papers upon which examinations are to be written shall be furnished by the Commission and shall bear some suitable official endorsement, stamp or mark.

10. On the day of the examination the identification sheets of candidates shall be sealed up, and the identity of each shall remain hidden until the papers are rated.

11. No candidate shall be granted a second or special examination or any second or special trial or test, either written or physical preliminary to or in connection with any examination held hereunder; unless it be shown to the satisfaction of the Commission that his failure to appear for, or to gain admission to, or to complete such examination or test, was due to a manifest error or missake for which the Commission is responsible, the nature of which shall be set forth in its minutes, or that such failure was due to compulsory attendance before any Court or other public authority having the power to compel such attendance.

12. No person who has entered any examination for appointment to a competitive position and failed therein or who has with-

drawn therefrom, shall be admitted within nine months from the date of such examination to a new examination for the same position.

For reasons to be set forth in its minutes, this provision may be waived by the Commission, with relation to all such candidates in a given examination but not to any individual.

13. No person shall be admitted to an examination whose application therefor has not been presented and accepted under the conditions of Rule VIII.

14. The Commission may refuse to examine or, after examination, to certify, an applicant who is found to lack any of the established preliminary requirements for the examination or position for which he applies; or who is found physically unfit to perform the duties attaching to such position, or who is addicted to the habitual use of intoxicating beverages to excess; or who has been guilty of a crime or of infamous or notoriously disgraceful conduct; or who has within two years been dismissed from the public service for delinquency or misconduct; or who has intentionally made a false statement of any material fact, or practiced or attempted to practice any deception or fraud in his application, or in his examination, or in securing his eligibility or appointment.

Where action is taken under this clause the name of the person affected, if it be upon any list, shall, after due notice to such person, and an opportunity to be heard if he so desires, be stricken from such list.

Rule VIII.

FILING OF APPLICATIONS.

1. Applications for examination for positions in the Competitive Class shall be addressed to the Commission on a prescribed form, in the handwriting of the applicant, and accompanied by such certificates or other evidences as to citizenship, character, condition of health, education, previous employment, training and fitness as the Commission may require.

The statements of the applicant in these particulars shall be made under oath, properly attested.

2. Every application shall bear the certificate of four reputable citizens, whose residences or places of business are within the City of New York, to the effect that they have personally known the

applicant for not less than one year, that they have read his statements and believe them to be correct, and that they will, upon request, give such further facts concerning him as they may possess either for the files of the Commission or for the information of appointing officers.

If the previous occupation or employment of the applicant has been wholly or in part outside the City of New York the said certificates may be accepted, in the discretion of the Commission, from persons resident or engaged in business elsewhere; but no such certificate shall be accepted from a near relative of the applicant or from any person the character of whose business, in the judgment of the Commission, may disqualify him as a fit voucher.

3. The Commission shall, by regulation or otherwise, fix the limits of time between which applications for a given examination shall be presented; but such period shall in no case be less than one week, and there shall be not less than five days between the last date for the presentation of applications and the date of examination.

No application shall be accepted from any person who has failed to fill out properly the application form, or to furnish the required certificates or other preliminary evidences of fitness; or who is barred by any of the provisions of Clause 3 of Rule II. or of Clause 14 of Rule VII.; or who has already on file an application entitling him to enter the examination sought.

4. An application presented within the prescribed limits of time, but found to be defective, shall be suspended, and notification shall be given to the applicant of the particulars in which it requires correction. Such an application shall be accepted if corrected and returned five days before the date of examination, but not otherwise.

5. Applications when presented shall be dated, numbered and recorded in the order of their receipt. An application that has been accepted and filed shall not be returned for any reason to the applicant.

6. A person claiming rights of preference as a veteran shall file, with his application, proof of such veteranship and of his residence within the State of New York.

7. Application forms shall be furnished to intending applicants, upon personal or written request, at the office of the Commission, and shall be procurable there only.

Rule IX.

MARKING AND RATING.

1. The examination papers shall be rated, in each case, by at least two examiners assigned therefor, who shall review them separately, and after such rating is completed shall affix to each a mark expressing the average of their judgment, attested by their respective signatures or initials. The marking shall be strictly comparative and according to such standards of proficiency as the needs of the service may require. Each subject shall be marked upon a scale of 100, which shall represent the maximum possible attainment.

2. Every candidate who receives a general average marking of not less than 70 per cent., and who has received not less than 20 per cent. in any required subject, or not less than 75 per cent., in any technical subject, when the examination is for a position of scientific, professional or technical nature, shall be eligible for certification and appointment in the manner, and under the conditions, hereinafter prescribed.

The Commission may, by resolution, require a specified percentage of 70 or more on any non-technical subject in any examination.

3. Where the Chief Examiner is satisfied, through investigation made under his direction, or otherwise, that the general character or the reputation of a candidate whose papers have been marked is not good, or that he is debarred by any of the provisions of Clause 14 of Rule VII., the name of such candidate shall not be placed on any eligible list; but all action under this clause shall be reported in writing, with the reasons therefor, to the Commission and shall be subject to the Commission's approval. The burden of proof of good character shall be upon the candidate who may, where doubt exists, be required to furnish evidence thereof additional to the certificates required at the time of his application.

4. The Secretary, as early as practicable after the completion of an examination, shall notify each candidate therein of the rating he has received, and, if such rating be above the required minimum, of his comparative standing. He shall likewise notify any candidate who, though admitted to the examination, has been rejected for reasons other than failure to receive the required minimum, stating such reasons specifically. Any candidate receiving any such notice may personally inspect his examination papers, at any time, during

the office hours of the Commission, and in the presence of such officer or employee as the Commission from time to time may designate.

5. No examination paper or any part thereof, and no record of the results of a physical test, or any other record or statement rated as part of an examination, or in connection therewith, shall be subject to review, alterat on or rerating after the marks of the examiners have been registered or attested as required hereunder; except that the Commission, at any time within a year from the date of the certification of an examination, may correct any manifest error or mistake of marking or rating appearing in any such paper or record, the nature of which it shall set forth in its minutes; such correction, in any case, to be without prejudice to the status of any person previously appointed as a result of such examination.

Rule X.

ELIGIBLE LISTS.

1. The results of each examination shall be reported by the Chief Examiner to the Secretary, who shall enter the names of the persons passing, in the order of their average rating, on the proper list of eligibles; provided that the names of veterans so passing shall be entered, in the order of average rating, at the head of such list. The date of the establishment of a list shall be the date of such report.

2. When two or more eligibles on a list have the same average rating, preference in certification shall be determined by the order in which their applications were filed, or, if the examination be for promotion, by the order of their original appointment in the department or other division of the service in which the promotion occurs.

3. The term of an eligible list shall be not less than one year nor more than four years from the date of its establishment. An elig ble list that has been in force for one year, except for the position of temporary clerk, shall terminate whenever a new list is established under the same title, and, in case of a graded position, for the same grade or grades.

Persons whose names appear on a list about to be terminated shall be notified of the new examination, in the same manner that applicants therefor are notified, and shall be informed that, upon the establishment of the new list, their original eligibility shall cease.

4. All eligible lists shall be published, as early as may be practicable after their establishment, in the "City Record."

Rule XI.

CERTIFICATION AND APPOINTMENT.

1. Selections for appointment to all positions in the Competitive Class not filled by promotion, reduction, transfer or reinstatement shall, except as provided in Rule XII., be made in the following manner:

The appointing officer shall notify the Commission of the title of the position, the duties to be performed and the compensation to be paid. The Commission shall thereupon certify to such appointing officer from the eligible list most nearly appropriate to such position, and for the grade thereof, if in a graded service, the three names at the head thereof; provided that, except in the case of a veteran, no such name shall be certified more than three times to the same appointing officer for the same or a similar position, unless at such officer's request. The relative rating of each candidate shall be stated in the certification, and, if the appointing officer requests, the application and examination papers of each shall be submitted for his inspection, at the office of the Commission. Certification shall be made without regard to sex unless sex is specified in the requisition.

The appointing officer shall make selection, with reference solely to merit and fitness, from the three names certified, unless objection shall be made, and sustained by the Commission, to one or more of the persons named, for any of the reasons stated in paragraph 14 of Rule VII., in which case the certification of three names shall be completed by addition of the name or names next following upon the eligible list. If there be more than one vacancy to be filled, or if the Commission has reason to anticipate declinations, it may supplement the certification for the first selection by the addition of names of those next in order on the list; provided that selection shall be made singly and in each case from the three highest names remaining eligible and those only who have been actually entitled to consideration for selection shall be credited with certifications. In any such case the reason for such action shall be stated in the minutes.

2. The person selected shall be duly notified by the appointing officer, and, upon accepting and reporting for duty, shall receive from such officer a certificate of appointment for a probationary period of three months; *except for the position of Patrolman, where*

such period shall be six months. For temporary service in accordance with clauses 1 and 2 of Rule XII., such certificates of appointment shall be issued for a probationary period of fifteen days. If his conduct or capacity on probation be unsatisfactory to the appointing officer the probationer shall be notified in writing that at the end of such period he shall, for that reason, not be retained; his retention in the service otherwise shall be equivalent to permanent appointment. Veterans of the Civil War, honorably discharged from the military or the naval service of the United States, shall not be subject to such probation.

3. A probationer separated from the service for any reason other than fault or delinquency shall be restored to the eligible list from which he was selected, with the same relative standing, and the time during which he has actually served shall be deducted from the period of probation if he be again selected by the same appointing officer. When two or more persons selected from the same eligible list are serving as probationers under the same appointing officer, and a reduction of force is necessary, they shall be preferred for retention in the order of their original standing on such list.

4. The name of any person certified as eligible for a probationary appointment who shall decline such appointment shall be stricken from the list from which such certification is made unless such declination be for one of the following reasons:

(*a*) Residence in a borough other than that in which the duties are to be performed; (*b*) insufficiency of the compensation offered, if such compensation be lower than the amount or the maximum amount stated in the announcement of examination; or (*c*) temporary inability, physical or otherwise, the evidences of which must be acceptable to and approved by the Commission and set forth in its minutes.

The failure of an eligible person to respond within four days to an offer of appointment sent to his post-office address, shall be considered a declination.

A person certified for appointment from an eligible list resulting from an open, competitive or a promotion examination, or from a list of suspended employees prepared in accordance with rule XIII., paragraph 1, who declines the position by reason of insufficiency of the compensation offered shall not be again certified for a position at the same or any less compensation. When such declination results in the appointment of an eligible not originally entitled to certification, the compensation of such appointee shall not be increased within one year thereafter beyond the amount offered to any person so declining, unless the person or persons originally declining have received or declined appointment at the higher amount.

On notification from an appointing officer that a person named in a certification has declined appointment, and on receipt from such officer of such declination in writing, or of evidence of the failure of such person to respond to a notice properly sent, such certification shall be completed by addition of the name of the eligible next in order.

5. No certification shall remain in force for a longer period than fifteen days, nor in any case beyond the life of the eligible list from which certification is made. Until such certification has been exhausted or terminated no new certification shall be made for the same position, but the names of the persons certified may be certified for any similar position.

6. Every person selected for appointment shall be required to fill out and sign, in the presence of the appointing officer or his representative, an identification sheet, repeating the essential facts stated by him at the time of examination, which shall be forwarded to the Commission with the notice of appointment and filed with the appointee's application papers.

If a person who is not entitled to certification is certified, such certification shall, after due notification from the Commission to the appointing officer, be revoked.

Rule XII.

TEMPORARY AND EXCEPTIONAL APPOINTMENTS.

1. When services are to be rendered of a temporary character, and for a limited period, the appointing officer shall inform the Commission, stating the duration of such period, the rate of compensation and other conditions of employment, and may select for such employment one of the first three persons on the appropriate eligible list who, after due notice of the conditions, are willing to accept certification therefor; but successive temporary appointments under this clause shall be permitted only upon the request of the appointing officer for reasons to be approved by the Commission, and in no

case shall such appointments continue for a longer period than six months.

2. The Commission shall establish and maintain a separate eligible list of persons willing to accept temporary employment as clerks, under the conditions of the preceding clause. If the appointing officer shall certify that the services of a person appointed from such list have been satisfactory the name of such person shall, at the termination of such temporary employment, be placed on a preferred list, from which he shall be eligible for re-employment for any similar service, under the conditions of Clause 1 of Rule XIII.

When a sufficient number of temporary clerks cannot be secured from such list, or from any other appropriate list, additional clerks may be employed without examination, in the following cases; but the appointing officer in each such case shall report to the Commission the names of the persons so employed, the character of their previous occupation, the terms of their employment by him and the rate of compensation to be paid them:

(*a*) In the office of the Receiver of Taxes, Department of Finance, for the period between September 1 and January 1, of each year;

(*b*) In the office of the Collector of Assessments and Arrears, Department of Finance, for the period between August 15 and December 15 of each year;

(*c*) In the office of the Registrar of Water Rates, Department of Water Supply, Gas and Electricity, for the period between May 1 and August 1 of each year;

(*d*) In the office of the Bureau of Elections, at times of election or registration, for a period of not exceeding forty days.

3. Whenever there are urgent reasons for filling a vacancy in any permanent position in the Competitive Class, and there is no existing appropriate eligible list, the appointing officer may nominate a person to the Commission for non-competitive examination, and if such nominee shall be certified by the Chief Examiner as qualified, after such examination, he may be appointed, provisionally, to fill such vacancy until an appropriate eligible list is established. The competitive examination for such position shall, in such case, be ordered, in the manner provided by Rule VII., for a date not later than three weeks from the date of such provisional appointment. Such provisional appointment shall not continue for more than ten days after an appropriate list has been established, nor for a longer period, in any case, than two months; nor shall successive provisional appointments be made to the same position under this provision.

4. Where there is a vacancy of an emergency character in a position in the Competitive Class, and it is not practicable either to secure a person by certification from an eligible list or to conduct a non-competitive examination in the absence of such a list in time to meet such emergency, an appointment may be made without certification or examination, subject to the subsequent approval of the Commission, for a period not exceeding fifteen days; and such appointment may be renewed for only one additional period of fifteen days, subject, however, to the approval of the Commission.

5. Where there is a vacancy in any position in the Competitive Class demanding peculiar and exceptional qualifications of a scientific, professional or educational character, and upon satisfactory evidence that for specified reasons competition in such special case is not practicable, and that the position can best be filled by the selection of some designated person of high and recognized attainments in such qualities the Commission may suspend the provisions of the rules requiring competition in such case; but no such suspension shall be general in its application to such position.

6. The Commission may, by resolution, except from competitive examination any person engaged in private business who shall render any professional, scientific, technical or expert service of an occasional and exceptional character to any city officer, and the amount of whose compensation in any one year shall not exceed $750; provided that such limitation of compensation shall not apply to any person so employed by the Mayor or Corporation Counsel; and provided further, that the Commission may, by resolution approved by the Mayor and the State Civil Service Commission, suspend such limitation in other cases.

7. The Commission may, by resolution, except from competitive examination any person who is to be appointed for service in a locality outside the City of New York who is a resident of such locality, and when appointment for such service from an eligible list is found to be not practicable; but no such person shall be eligible for transfer or assignment to work within the city.

8. The Commission may except from examination any person engaged in private business who shall render services of a professional, scientific, technical or expert nature of an occasional and exceptional character rendered under an agreement or contract to perform certain specified work, and who is not regularly or continuously employed by The City of New York, and where it appears

that the work to be performed is of such a character that no definite estimate can be given as to limit of time or compensation.

9. All exceptions from competitive examinations under this rule, with the circumstances thereof, shall be stated by the Commission in its annual report.

Rule XIII.

SUSPENSION AND REINSTATEMENT.

1. Whenever any permanent position in the Competitive Class is abolished or made unnecessary, or whenever the number of positions of a certain character is reduced, the person or persons legally holding such positions shall be deemed to be suspended without pay, and the names of such persons shall, on due notification from the appointing officer, be placed by the Commission on a special list, under such classified title and corresponding to such competitive eligible list as, in the judgment of the Commission, most nearly cover the class of duties performed by such persons in the position from which suspension is made; but no person who has received a permanent appointment shall be suspended from any position for lack of work or appropriation while probationers serving under the same title are employed in the same department, office or institution. For a period of one year from the date of suspension such persons shall be entitled to reinstatement in any position, or any grade of such position, for which certification from such corresponding eligible list might be made, and the Secretary shall certify their names to the proper appointing officer as entitled to such reinstatement, in the order of the dates of their original appointment to the Classified Service, before certification is made from such corresponding eligible list for any such vacancy; provided that such persons shall be selected for certification, *first*, for a position the same as that from which suspension was made, if the vacancy exists in such a position, and *second*, for corresponding or similar positions.

A person so certified who declines to accept reinstatement, except for one of the reasons and under the conditions stated in subdivision 4 of Rule XI., shall be considered to be permanently separated from the service.

2. The provisions of the foregoing clause shall not apply to any person who resigns his position or who is suspended or removed therefrom for any reason other than those therein specified.

3. A person who has resigned from a permanent competitive position, or who has been removed or otherwise separated therefrom for any cause other than fault or delinquency on his part, may be reinstated without examination, at any time within one year from the date of such separation, in a vacant position in the same class and grade, provided that for original entrance to such position there is not required by these rules, in the judgment of the Commission, an examination involving tests or qualifications different from or higher than those involved in the examination for appointment to the position formerly held by such person. But no person shall be so reinstated who at any time within a year prior to the date of his separation from the service had been eligible for reinstatement as a suspended employee.

The Commission may in its discretion extend the period during which reinstatement may be made under this clause where the person seeking reinstatement resigned his position in order to serve in the Army or Navy of the United States in time of war, and has received an honorable discharge therefrom.

4. Upon the written request of an appointing officer, stating the essential facts regarding a reinstatement proposed under the foregoing clause, the Commission will, if such reinstatement be in accordance with law and these rules, issue its certificate to that effect to such officer, but no such reinstatement shall be made or recognized until after the issuance of such certificate.

Rule XIV.

TRANSFER.

1. A person who has been permanently appointed to a position in the Competitive Class may be transferred without examination to a similar position in such class, or to a position within the same grade thereof, if it be in a graded service, in any other department, office or institution; provided, that for original entrance to the position proposed to be filled by transfer there is not required by these rules, in the judgment of the Commission, an examination involving tests or qualifications essentially different from or higher than those required in an examination for original entrance to the position from which transfer is sought; and provided further,

that if such person entered the service without competitive examination he shall have served with fidelity for at least three years in the position held by him, or in a similar position.

2. A person may be transferred from an exempt or non-competitive position to a competitive position, or from a position in the Competitive Class to a position in a different group of such class, only when the person transferred has qualified in an open competitive examination and is eligible for certification and appointment from the appropriate eligible list for the position to which transfer is proposed. Such transfer shall remove from the eligible list the name of the person transferred; but no such transfer shall be allowed when there is in existence an appropriate list of persons eligible for promotion to the position proposed to be filled by transfer.

A person holding a position in the Non-Competitive Class may be transferred to a similar position in the same class.

3. A person who has been permanently appointed to a position in the competitive class in any department, and who was separated from his position in that class by appointment to a position in the non-competitive or exempt class, or to a position in another group of the competitive class, and who has served continuously therein from the date of such separation may be restored without the application of the foregoing restrictions, either to the position originally held by him, or to any position to which transfer could be made therefrom.

4. Upon the written request of an appointing officer, stating the facts with reference to a proposed transfer, accompanied by the consent, also in writing, of the person to be transferred and of the appointing officer from whose jurisdiction the transfer is to be made, the Commission may, if such transfer be in accordance with law and the provisions of these rules, issue its certificate to that effect; but no such transfer shall be made or recognized until after the issuance of such certificate.

Rule XV.

PROMOTION.

1. Vacancies in positions above the lowest grade in any part of the Competitive Class, except Part I., that are not filled by original appointment, transfer, reinstatement or reduction, shall be filled by promotion, based, so far as practicable, on competitive tests.

2. Examinations for promotion shall be ordered as often as may be necessary to meet or anticipate the needs of the higher grades, and, so far as practicable, shall be held periodically. Such examinations shall be open to all persons otherwise eligible who shall have served the necessary periods as particularly described below.

3. Mental examinations for promotion shall, as far as practicable, correspond in scope, subjects and preliminary conditions to examinations as would have been prescribed for original entrance to the same position, but due consideration shall be given to the particular requirements of the department, office or institution for which the examination is held. No person shall be eligible for promotion who lacks any of the preliminary requirements for original entrance to the position to be filled by promotion.

4. No examination shall be held under any title not designated in the classifications, except that, for reasons to be stated in its minutes, the Commission may hold an examination under the office title of a position above Grade 4 of the Clerical Service, where the duties to be performed are of a fixed and distinctive character, and where such office title has been in common use for not less than a year.

5. No person shall be admitted to an examination for promotion who lacks any preliminary qualification for the position to be filled, fixed by law or by these rules or by lawful regulation of his department, or who may have become ineligible for any of the causes set forth in Clause 14 of Rule VII.

6. Eligibility for promotion shall be limited to persons who have served for not less than six months immediately preceding the examination in the department, office or institution for which the examination is held. Promotion examinations in all parts of the competitive class shall be further regulated as particularly described below.

7. Part I.—Ungraded Positions—Whenever a vacancy exists or is anticipated in a position in Part I., which, in the opinion of the appointing officer or of the Commission, can be filled satisfactorily by promotion from among persons holding positions of lower but corresponding character in the same Part, the Commission may order a competitive examination for such promotion, open to all persons who shall have served with fidelity for not less than one year in such lower position.

8. Part II.—The Clerical Service—

(*a*) All persons who shall have served with fidelity for not less than one year in positions in Grade 1, and not less than two years in positions in Grade 2, and not less than three years in positions in Grades 3 and 4, shall be eligible for examination for the next higher grade in the same position.

(*b*) The Commission may extend eligibility for promotion to any position in Part II. to persons who have served the required length of time in the grade in another group in Part II. when the Commission shall find that the nature of the duties of the positions held by such persons are such as naturally and properly fit them to perform the duties of the position to which they seek promotion.

(*c*) Upon the request of an appointing officer the Commission may authorize an examination for change of title within a grade for any position in Part II. from among persons holding positions of lower but corresponding character in the same grade. Such examinations shall be limited to persons who have served at least one year in such lower position.

(*d*) The Commission may extend eligibility for promotion to positions in Grade 2 of Part II. to persons who shall have served at least two years; and to Grade 3 of Part II. to persons who shall have served at least five years in positions in Part VI. (the Attendant Service), where the Commission shall find that the duties of the positions held by such persons are such as naturally and properly fit them to perform the duties of the positions to which they seek promotion, as fully as the duties of persons otherwise eligible under this rule.

9. Part III.—The Engineering Service—Examinations shall be open to all persons who shall have served with fidelity for not less than six months in positions in the same class in the grade next lower in the same department, office or institution. For increase of salary in the same position beyond the grades fixed by these rules, examinations shall be open to all persons who shall have served with fidelity for not less than six months in the grade next lower.

10. Parts IV., the Inspection Service; V., the Legal Service; VI., the Attendance Service, and XII., the Medical Service—Wherever a vacancy exists or is anticipated in a position in Parts IV., V., VI. and XII., which, in the opinion of the appointing officer or of the Commission, may be filled satisfactorily by promotion from among persons holding positions of lower but corresponding character in the same part, the Commission may order a competitive examination for such promotion open to all persons who shall have served at least one year in such lower position. For increase of salary in the same position beyond the grades fixed by these rules, examinations shall be open to all persons who shall have served with fidelity for not less than six months in the grade next lower.

11. Part VII., the Police Service; Part VIII., the Fire Service—Examinations for promotion shall be held in accordance with Rule XVII. When promotions to positions are limited by law to persons serving a definite length of time in certain grades, a person to be eligible for examination must have completed such length of service not later than the day of the mental examination for the position. Where no requirements of law exist as to length of service, examinations shall be open in each case to all persons who shall have served for not less than six months in positions of the same general character in the grade next lower.

12. Part IX.—The Prison Service—Persons who shall have served with fidelity for not less than five years in Grade 1 shall be eligible for examination for promotion to Grade 2. Persons who shall have served at least six months in Grades 2 and 3 shall be eligible for promotion to the next higher grade.

13. Part X.—The Street Cleaning Service—Examinations shall be open to all persons who shall have served with fidelity for not less than six months in positions of the same general character in the grade next lower.

14. Part XI.—The Ferry Service—Examinations shall be open to all persons who shall have served with fidelity for not less than six months in positions in the same class in the grade next lower.

15. A position in any of the aforesaid parts, the compensation of which is not identical with that specified in the classification for any grade of such parts, shall for purposes of promotion, be deemed as of the grade the compensation of which is specified as next lower than the compensation paid.

16. For reasons to be set forth in its minutes and where permitted by law and under the restriction fixed by these rules relative to promotion from one grade to the next higher, the Commission may open examinations to persons in two or more lower grades who shall have served with fidelity for the required time in the lowest grade to which the examination is open.

17. Whenever a vacancy exists or is anticipated in a position in Part I. or in the lowest graded positions of Parts III., IV., X. and XI., or in grades 1 and 2 of Part VI. which, in the opinion of the appointing officer or of the Commission, can be filled satisfactorily by the promotion of persons employed in a position of lower but corresponding character in the labor class, the Commission may,

by resolution, order a competitive examination for such promotion open to all persons who have served with fidelity for not less than three years in such lower position.

18. Whenever a vacancy exists or is anticipated in a position in the Competitive Class which at a lower compensation is classified in the Non-Competitive Class, the Commission shall, if, in its opinion, the vacancy can practically be filled by the promotion of persons employed in such position of lower salary but corresponding character in the Non-Competitive Class, order a competitive examination for such promotion, open to all persons who have served with fidelity for not less than three years in such lower position.

19. For reasons to be stated in its minutes, and where permitted by law, the Commission may extend eligibility for promotion to positions appearing in Part I., The Ungraded Service; Part III., The Engineering Service; Part IV., The Inspection Service; Part V., The Legal Service; Part VI., The Attendance Service, and Part XII., The Medical Service, to persons who have served in positions appearing in another part of the classification where it shall find that the nature of the duties of the positions held by such persons is such as naturally and properly fit them to perform the duties of the positions to which they seek promotion, as fully as do the duties of persons who are eligible for examination, as otherwise provided by these rules.

In determining eligiblity for such promotion, the titles of positions in themselves, and the duties which are naturally and properly attached thereto shall be considered. Duties which have been performed not in accordance with the title of the position, or alleged personal qualifications, shall not be considered in determining such eligibility.

20. The subjects of rating and the relative weights thereof in any competitive promotion examination shall be as follows: For comparative conduct, seniority and efficiency in previous service, as may be determined from the transcript of the efficiency record (or as may be otherwise determined under paragraph 21 of this rule), between the date of the original appointment of the candidate and the final date for the receiving of applications for any stated examination, 50; and for written papers on pertinent subjects, 50. (In cases where the candidate has obtained a promotion as the result of a competitive examination, the record shall be a continuation of the last record furnished; but if the promotion be obtained without

competitive examination, the record shall commence from the date of his promotion to the position or grade).

In rating records where more than one grade is opened, such rating shall be based upon the service of a candidate in all of such positions or grades.

21. To provide a basis of rating for previous service, there shall be kept in each department or office continuous and permanent records of the efficiency, character and conduct of all persons employed in "positions in the competitive class." Such records shall be known as "efficiency records," and the entries made therein shall have reference to (*a*) quality of work performed by each officer or employee; (*b*) the quantity of work performed by him; (*c*) his general conduct; (*d*) his punctuality and attendance; (*e*) his executive ability and capacity for initiative where his work is of a character that will permit definite estimation.

22. The entries upon an efficiency record shall be made under the direction of a board of promotions to be established in each department which shall consist of not less than three superior officers or employees of such department, who shall be designated for such purpose by the appointing officer therein, subject to confirmation by the Commission. Such entries shall be based upon reports submitted by the administrative officer most closely in touch with the work of the officer or employee to be rated, and shall be made quarterly on or about the first day of January, April, July and October of each year and shall be a record for the quarter immediately preceding. Such reports shall be made on a form to be prescribed by the Commission. After the board of promotions has passed upon the terms to be used to indicate the degree of efficiency of the several employees, the original reports and the recommendations made in accordance shall be transmitted to the Commission for its approval before any entries are made upon the efficiency record. Whenever, in the judgment of the Commission, more exact information is required than that given in such reports, the original records of the department may be consulted or such other action taken as may be deemed advisable. The Commission shall have power to change or amend any of the recommendations made by the boards of promotions as to the terms to be used to indicate degrees of efficiency, where it shall find that such terms are not warranted by the reports submitted or that such reports do not contain a fair and true account of the comparative efficiency of the several employees whose names appear therein. Where such

changes are made the reasons shall be given in writing to the department concerned. When the Commission has considered the recommendations made in the reports, it shall transmit an account of its findings to the several departments, after which the entries shall be made upon the efficiency records. The following terms shall be employed to indicate the degree of efficiency; (*a*) Far above the average; (*b*) above the average; (*c*) average; (*d*) below the average; (*e*) far below the average. For periods of service prior to the establishment, or in the absence of any such record, such ratings shall be based on such certificates, covering the several elements of service herein specified, in such forms as the Commission may require. The efficiency records shall be open to either the Chief Examiner or to any examiner designated by him, and, at reasonable times, to any officer or employee whose conduct is noted therein.

23. Any person in the competitive service who shall have obtained his position as the result of an examination either for appointment or promotion covering in its scope a higher grade or compensation than that of the position he holds may be promoted to such higher grade or compensation without further examination, with the consent of the Commission, provided that the eligible list through which he received his appointment has been promulgated within four years preceding the date of such promotion; that there is not more than one other person in the same position and the same grade in the bureau or other sub-division of the department in which the promotion is to be made, and that he has actually served at least one year in the said bureau or other sub-division. The bureau or other sub-division of the department, within the meaning of this paragraph, shall be an entirely separate sub-division of the department, recognized as such by the Commission.

24. A person whose grade or compensation has at any time been reduced may, by order of the Commission, be restored to such grade or compensation without further examination, provided that such restoration does not involve a change in the duties of the person to be promoted.

25. No recommendation for the promotion of any person in the classified service shall be considered by any officer concerned in making promotions unless it shall be made by an officer under whose supervision such person has served; such recommendation by any other person, if made with the knowledge and consent of the person to whom it relates, shall be sufficient cause for debarring such person

from the promotion proposed, and a repetition of the offense shall be sufficient cause for his removal.

26. Except as this rule otherwise provides, the conduct of an examinat on for promotion and the making of selections therefor from any eligible list formed as the result of such examination, shall be governed by the rules relating to original appointment.

Rule XVI.

REMOVALS.

1. No person holding a position in the service of the city shall be removed from such position, except in the manner prescribed by the Charter and the Civil Service Law; and the officer charged with the power of removal, in each case, shall transmit to the Commission, with the report of his action required under Rule XX., a copy of the reasons therefor, or of the findings of any trial board or officer, as stated to the person removed, and as filed in the department or office.

2. No person who is an honorably discharged soldier, sailor or marine, having served as such in the Union Army or Navy during the War of the Rebellion, or in the Army or Navy of the United States during the Spanish War, or who is a veteran volunteer fireman, shall be removed from any position in the classified service except in the manner prescribed by section 21 of the Civil Service Law.

3. The provisions of this rule shall apply to the removal of any person from a graded position by reduction to a position in a lower grade, but shall not apply to a suspension from service for lack of work or reduction of force.

Rule XVII.

SPECIAL PROVISIONS AFFECTING THE POLICE AND FIRE SERVICES.

1. Before admission to an examination for the Police or the Fire Service, each applicant therefor, whose application has been accepted, shall be subjected to medical and physical tests having reference to (*a*) measurements of weight, height and chest expansion and mobility; (*b*) sight and hearing; (*c*) habits as to the use

of stimulants and narcotics; (*d*) general organic condition, and (*e*) previous condition of health. The medical and physical examiners shall report to the Commission in writing the results of such tests, and no applicant shall be admitted to the examination who is not certified by them to be qualified and sound in each of the aforesaid particulars.

2. The minimum relative measurements required shall be as follows:

FIREMEN.		FIREMEN and PATROLMEN.		PATROLMEN.	
Expansion.	Mobility.	Height.	Weight.	Expansion.	Mobility.
36½ inches.	3 inches.	5 feet 7½ inches.	140 pounds.	36½ inches.	3 inches.
36½ "	3 "	5 " 8 "	140 "	36½ "	3 "
37 "	3½ "	5 " 9 "	145 "	37 "	3½ "
37 "	3½ "	5 " 10 "	150 "	37 "	3½ "
37½ "	3½ "	5 " 11 "	155 "	37½ "	3½ "
37½ "	4 "	6 " .. "	160 "	37½ "	4 "
38 "	4 "	6 " 1 "	165 "	38 "	4 "
38 "	4 "	6 " 2 "	170 "	38 "	4 "
38 "	4 "	6 " 3 "	175 "	38 "	4 "
38 "	4½ "	6 " 4 "	180 "	38 "	4½ "
38 "	4½ "	6 " 5 "	185 "	38 "	4½ "

3. A candidate to be eligible for appointment must obtain an average of not less than 70 per cent. on the mental tests and 70 per cent. on the physical development and strength. Candidates for the Fire Department who obtain an average of over 80 per cent. on the physical development and strength and a final average of 75 per cent. shall also be eligible for appointment.

4. No candidate shall be eligible for promotion whose ascertained general average is less than 80 per cent.

5. Whenever a position in either the Police or the Fire Service to which promotion is sought calls for qualifications of a special or technical character, the Chief Examiner may, subject to the direction of the Commission, fix such subjects therefor as may be appropriate, in addition to those required for the promotion in grade; but such subjects shall conform as nearly as possible to those set for similar positions in other parts of the Competitive Class.

6. The positions of Engineer of Steamer and Pilot, in Grade 1 of the Fire Service, shall be filled by special competitive examination, open to all firemen of the first grade as defined by section 740 of the City Charter.

7. In every particular not herein specified appointments or promotions in the Police or the Fire Service are subject to the general provisions of these rules.

Rule XVIII.

THE NON-COMPETITIVE CLASS.

1. The positions in the Non-Competitive Class shall be those of a minor nature, in the city institutions or elsewhere, that it is not practicable to fill either through competition or through registration under the provisions of Rule XIX., and that are specifically designated in the classification.

2. In each department or institution where there are positions in the non-competitive class, there shall be a Board of Examiners for such positions, composed of not less than three superior officers or employees of such department or institution, who shall be designated by the Appointing Officer therein, subject to confirmation by the Commission.

3. A vacancy in any position in the said class, at compensation not exceeding the limit, if any, set in the classification for such position, may be filled by the appointment of any person who, upon nomination by the appointing officer to such Board of Examiners, and upon appropriate non-competitive examination, shall be certified by such Board to be qualified to perform the duties of such position. In any department or institution having a number of such employees in the same class of work, the appointing officer, in order to provide a list permitting immediate selection, in case of necessity may nominate for examination more than one person, but selection shall be made, in such a case, in the order of the placing of the names upon such list.

4. Such examinations shall be conducted so as to show (*a*) that the applicant is free from any physical defect likely to interfere with the proper discharge of his duties; (*b*) that his general character and habits are satisfactory, and (*c*) that he possesses the requisite knowledge and ability, or that he is qualified by experience to discharge his duties efficiently and intelligently.

5. For the position of Trained Nurse, when the applicant is a Registered Nurse, under chapter 293 of the Laws of 1903, a certificate of such registry may, when presented, be accepted in lieu of the examination required herein, and for the position of Master, Mate or Pilot, the certificate or license of the United States Steamboat Inspection Bureau may be accepted in lieu of such examination.

6. The Commission shall supervise and regulate the conduct of examinations by the Boards of Examiners, and may prescribe uniform conditions and tests of fitness for the guidance and government of the Examiners.

7. Each Board of Examiners shall transmit to the Commission at the end of each month a statement of the results of the examinations they have conducted, setting forth the names of the persons examined or appointed, the compensation of each, and such other information as the Commission may require.

8. Any position of which the title appears in the classification of the Non-Competitive Class, but with compensation attaching thereto which exceeds the limit, if any, set by the classification for such position shall be deemed to be in either the Competitive or the Labor Class, according to the duties of such position.

9. No person holding a position in the Non-Competitive Class shall be increased in compensation beyond the limit set in the classification for such position unless he shall have qualified for appointment for such higher paid position in an open competitive examination or shall have been promoted in accordance with paragraph 18 of Rule XV.

10. For the purpose of these rules, maintenance is established at $180 per annum. A person appointed without maintenance may in the discretion of the appointing officer be granted maintenance, provided his compensation with maintenance does not exceed $180 less than the limit fixed for the position without maintenance, and a person appointed with maintenance may be continued in the same position without maintenance provided his compensation does not exceed $180 more than the limit fixed for the position with maintenance.

Rule XIX.

THE LABOR CLASS.

1. Positions in the Labor Class that are not filled through transfer or reinstatement shall be filled by selection, in the manner

hereinafter provided from among those persons whose names are highest on the most nearly appropriate eligible list, resulting from the registration, according to priority of application, of duly qualified applicants therefor.

2. The Commission shall establish, and so far as practicable, shall maintain continuously, registration lists of persons eligible for employment under each title in the Labor Class, and, where the character of the position requires, may establish separate lists under such titles for each borough and for the counties of Westchester, Putnam, Dutchess, Ulster and Nassau; but a person certified and employed from a borough or county list shall not be eligible for transfer or assignment to work in any other borough or county within six months from the date of such employment.

3. For the purposes of such registration, and of the qualifying examinations required, the Labor Class shall be subdivided as follows:

Part I.—Laborers and others registered for employment in a designated borough or county.

Part II.—Mechanics and others registered for employment in any borough.

Part III.—Mechanics registered for employment in any borough, subject to trade examination.

Part IV.—Laborers and Mechanics registered for employment in hospitals.

The positions included in each of the aforesaid subdivisions shall be those so designated in the Classification.

4. Applications for registration for positions in the Labor Class shall be addressed to the Commission on a prescribed form, signed by the applicant with his name or mark, indicating the position sought, stating, under oath, such facts as to his age, residence, citizenship, physical condition, previous occupation and experience as the Commission may require, and accompanied by the certificate of three reputable citizens, whose residences or places of business are within the City of New York or within the county in which he resides, to the effect that they have known him personally for not less than one year, that they believe his character and habits of industry and sobriety to be good, and that they have read his statements and believe them to be correct. If the applicant has been employed, at least one of such persons shall be an employer or former employer, who shall certify as to his capacity for the kind of work for which he applies, or an explanation satisfactory to the

Commission shall be given as to why such a certificate cannot be obtained. If the application is not in the handwriting of the applicant, he shall state by whom it was written, giving the name, occupation and address of such person.

When the applicant desires to be registered for employment in any recognized trade, he shall state the number of years of his general experience as a journeyman in such trade, and shall present, in addition to the certificates aforesaid, a certificate signed by a firm, or member thereof by which he has been employed in such trade, or by a superintendent or master workman, still in the service of such firm, under whom he has worked therein, vouching for his practical capacity and fitness as a mechanic.

No certificate required under this clause shall be based upon previous employment in a city department unless signed both by the head of such department, and by the officer under whose personal supervision the services, in such case, were performed.

The classification of positions in the Labor Class and the text of this rule shall be printed, for the information of applicants, on the blank form of application, and copies of such form shall be procurable, on the personal or written request of the applicant, at the Application Bureau of the Commission only.

5. Applications for a given position shall be received either continuously or between fixed dates, as the Commission may by regulation or resolution require; but no such fixed period shall be of less duration than two weeks and public notice thereof shall be given so far as practicable, in the manner prescribed for a position in the Competitive Class.

6. On the receipt of an application properly filled out and attested, and accompanied by the required certificates, a number shall be affixed thereto, showing the order of such receipt, and the name of the applicant shall be recorded in such order. As often as may be necessary to meet or to anticipate the needs of the service, such applicants shall be notified, in the order of application, to appear for physical examination, at such time and place as the Commission may require. The number called for such examination shall be sufficient to provide an adequate registration list, but shall in no case be less than fifty, if that number have applied. No application when filed shall be subject to change, or be returned to the applicant for any reason.

7. On appearing for the physical examination applicants shall be questioned concerning the statements made in their application blanks and concerning their previous employment and experience. If the answers made are in any important respect at variance with such statements, examination in such case shall be suspended, and if it appears on investigation, or through information otherwise received, that such applicant has willfully made a false statement or that he has connived at any false statement made in any certificate, his name shall be removed from any list on which it appears, and he shall be disqualified thereafter for either examination or registration.

An applicant who fails to report for physical examination, when duly notified, shall lose his application number, but his name may, in the discretion of the Commission, be again recorded, without renewal of his application, if a request in writing, stating the reasons for such failure, be presented not later than ten days thereafter.

8. The physical examination shall have reference generally to (*a*) measurements of weight and height; (*b*) sight and hearing; (*c*) habits as to the use of stimulants and narcotics; (*d*) general organic condition, and (*e*) previous condition of health; and, particularly, to such qualities of strength or endurance as may be important in the kind of work to be performed.

Where practicable, and when in the judgment of the Commission an examination, either oral or practical, is required for any position in Part I. or II., the same may be held in conjunction with the physical examination, and any applicant failing to meet the required standard shall be rejected.

For positions in Part III. applicants shall be subjected, further, to practical tests of skill and capacity in the use of the tools of their trade.

The Commission may prescribe limits of age for any position where, in its judgment, the nature of the work to be performed demands, and subject to the provisions of law respecting veterans.

9. The names of those persons who are certified by the examiners to be physically qualified for the employment sought, and, where the position is in Part III., to be qualified in their respective trades, shall be entered upon the appropriate registration list in the order of original application; except that the names of veterans, thus qualified, shall be placed at the head of such list, in the order of application.

No person shall remain eligible for selection for employment from such list who, on the first day of January, April, July or October, in any year, has been carried thereon for one year or longer; but the Commission may, by request, and in its discretion, allow a re-examination of all such persons, physically, at the termination of any period of their eligibility, and if they shall again be qualified, as the result of such examination, their names shall be retained on such list for one year from such quarterly date.

No application shall remain in force which, on any such date, has run for two years or longer without a call for examination; unless, with the consent of the Commission, it be renewed for a further period of two years.

10. When the services of laborers are required in any department, office or institution, the appointing officer thereof shall notify the Commission, stating the character of the work to be performed, the place of employment, the number of persons required, the wages to be paid and the probable duration of such employment. The Commission shall thereupon certify from the appropriate list the names of those standing highest thereon, and except as herein provided, such certification, and appointments or selections for employment therefrom, shall be made in the manner prescribed by Rule XI. for positions in the Competitive Class. The name of any person certified as eligible for employment from a county list in connection with the water supply who shall decline such employment shall be stricken from the list from which such certification is made, unless such declination be for the reason of residence in a township other than that in which the duties are to be performed.

11. In a case of emergency, where it is not practicable to secure laborers from an eligible list with sufficient promptness, or where a list is temporarily exhausted, an appointing officer may hire and employ for a period not exceeding five days as many persons as may be required, but he shall in such case report his action, with full particulars thereof, to the Commission, and such action shall be subject to the Commission's subsequent approval.

In case of extraordinary emergency involving the public welfare, and where the appropriate eligible lists are exhausted, the Commission may authorize the extension of such employment, but the reasons therefor, with the full particulars thereof, must be stated in its minutes.

12. It shall be the duty of an appointing officer to submit in such manner as the Commission may prescribe the report of appointments and changes in the Labor Class required by law, and upon the termination of an employment he shall in each case certify to the Commission the reasons therefor. Where such termination is due to a reduction of force the name of the person affected, if he has been employed for a period of one month or less, shall be restored to the registration list, in its original relative order; if such person has been employed for a longer period than one month, he shall be deemed to be suspended from such employment, and shall be registered upon a preferred list for reinstatement, if his services be again required, in the manner prescribed by Clause 1 of Rule XIII. for positions in the Competitive Class. Any necessary reduction of force shall be made from among those persons who have not been employed for a period of one month, persons who have completed their probationary period having preference for retention.

No person whose employment is terminated for the reason of failure to work, incompetence, or physical or moral unfitness shall be eligible for re-registration for a period of six months from the date of such termination, and then only upon furnishing to the Commission a satisfactory explanation of his failure to work, or satisfactory evidence that such other disqualification no longer exists.

A person employed in a Labor position under these rules, who after three months' service in such position, left it voluntarily, and without fault or delinquency on his part, may be re-employed in the same position, within one year of the date of his separation, without further examination or registration if there be no persons eligible for reinstatement upon a preferred list for such position.

13. A person who has served in a department or institution with fidelity for one year in a position in the Labor Class may be transferred to any other position in said class for which he may be shown to possess such qualifications, in respect either to previous experience or to physical or technical fitness, as may be required in the case of original appointment to such other position, on the issuance by the Commission of a certificate to such effect for service in such department or institution. Any employee in the Labor Class may be transferred from one department or institution to any other department or institution, under the same title, provided that he has served in the department or institution from which transfer is sought for

a period of one month, and provided further, that no one has been suspended for lack of work or appropriation from the department or institution to which transfer is to be made; but no person shall be transferred from an office in one borough or county to any other borough or county until he shall have served for a period of six months in the borough or county from which transfer is to be made. No person shall be otherwise transferred or assigned to the duties of a different position, except that in the Department of Street Cleaning, during the winter season, persons in the uniformed force may be detailed in emergencies for clerical service in the offices of the Snow and Ice Bureau.

14. Where, through the operation of these rules, the title of an existing registration list is discontinued, the names of persons thereon shall be placed upon such other existing list as the Commission, by resolution, may declare to be most appropriate, in the same order, with relation to other names upon such list, as though they had been originally registered thereon.

Rule XX.

THE CIVIL LIST AND REPORTS OF CHANGES IN THE SERVICE.

1. The Commission shall keep in its office an official roster of the Classified City Service, which shall be known as the "Civil List," and a transcript of which, omitting the names of persons in the Labor or the Non-Competitive Class, and of date of December 31 of each year, shall be published in the "City Record" during the month of January following. The Commission shall enter upon such roster the name of every person who has been appointed to or employed, promoted or reinstated in any position in such service, upon such evidence as it may require or deem satisfactory, that such person was appointed, employed, promoted or reinstated in conformity with the provisions of law and of these rules. Such roster shall show opposite or in connection with each name placed thereon the date of appointment, employment, promotion or reinstatement, the compensation of the position, the date of commencement of service, and the date of transfer in or of separation from the service by suspension, removal, resignation, cancellation of appointment or death. Such roster shall also bear the residence by street num-

bers where there are such, of each such person, which shall be corrected when such residence is changed, on notice from the said person in writing.

2. In preparing the transcript of such roster for publication, or for transmission with its annual report to the State Civil Service Commission, the Commission shall summarize the number of persons employed in the Labor and in the Non-Competitive Class respectively, and, as accurately as practicable, the details of such employment, and, before publishing or transmitting such roster, shall append thereto a copy of such summary. In connection with such annual publication in the "City Record," the Commission shall publish also a separate statement, giving by departments, the names of all persons whose official status has been changed during the year covered, either by promotion or reduction, or by increase or decrease of compensation, and showing, in each case, the date of such change, the titles of positions interchanged, the differences in salary, and, in cases of advance in status, whether such advance was based upon examination under these rules.

3. It shall be the duty of each appointing officer to report to the Commission in writing each selection made by him for appointment to, or employment or reinstatement in, any position in the Classified Service, except in the Non-Competitive Class, upon the date thereof, stating, in each case, the name of the appointee or employee, the title and character of his office or employment, the date of commencement of service by virtue thereof, and the amount of compensation to be paid; and it shall be the duty of such officer to report to the Commission, in like manner, upon the date of his official action therein or knowledge thereof, in each case, every suspension, removal or resignation from, or transfer to, any such position, with such pertinent data with relation to each as the Commission may require.

Rule XXI.

CERTIFICATION OF PAY-ROLLS.

1. It shall be the duty of the appointing officer in any department, office or institution the employees of which are paid direct from the treasury of the city to submit to the Commission all payrolls for certification, as required by section 19 of the Civil Service Law, and to certify to the Commission that the persons named

therein were appointed or promoted to, or employed in the positions indicated, in compliance with the provisions of the Civil Service Law and of these rules, and that they are regularly employed in the performances of the appropriate duties of such indicated positions, and have at no time during the period covered by such pay-roll been assigned to the performance of duties appertaining to any other title.

The duties herein prescribed to be done by the appointing officer may be performed by another officer of the department duly designated by the appointing officer for that purpose.

2. All pay-rolls shall, before transmission to the Comptroller or other fiscal officer of the city, bear the certificate of the Commission that the persons whose names appear thereon have been appointed or employed or promoted in pursuance of the Civil Service Law and of these rules. Such pay-rolls shall in each case be verified by comparison with the official roster, and if it appears that any person whose name is borne thereon has been appointed or employed, or continued in employment, in any manner contrary to the provisions of law or of these rules, such certification, in the case of such person, shall be denied.

The Commission, by resolution, may authorize the Secretary, the Assistant Secretary or the Chief Clerk to attach the certificate herein required.

Rule XXII.

TRANSMISSION OF RULES.

The Commission shall transmit a certified copy of these rules within ten days of their promulgation to each board or officer having power of appointment to any office or position in the City Service, and in like manner to each such officer who may hereafter be elected or appointed, on the assumption of the duties and authority of his office.

APPENDIX: CLASSIFICATION

APPENDIX

CLASSIFICATION OF THE CIVIL SERVICE

THE EXEMPT CLASS

ACCOUNTS, COMMISSIONER OF

Director, Standard Testing Laboratory
Efficiency Engineer
17 Examiners of Accounts
2 Examining Inspectors
2 Examining Engineers
2 Stenographers to Commissioners

ARMORY BOARD

Secretary of the Board

ART COMMISSION

Assistant Secretary

BOARD OF ASSESSORS

Secretary of the Board
Stenographer to the Board

BOARD OF INEBRIETY

Executive Secretary

BELLEVUE AND ALLIED HOSPITALS

Secretary to the President
5 Assistant Superintendents of Training School
General Superintendent of Training School
Superintendent of Training School
8 Chaplains

BOROUGH PRESIDENT IN EACH BOROUGH, OFFICE OF THE

Secretary of the Borough
Stenographer to the President
Confidential Inspector
Secretary to the President—Manhattan, Brooklyn, Queens and The Bronx

BRIDGES, DEPARTMENT OF

Deputy Commissioner
Chief Engineer
4 Consulting Engineers
Secretary to the Commissioner
Secretary of the Department

BROOKLYN DISCIPLINARY TRAINING SCHOOL

Superintendent

3 Chaplains

BUILDINGS, BUREAU OF, IN EACH BOROUGH

Superintendent of Buildings
Asst. Supt. of Buildings
Stenographer to Superintendent, Manhattan
Consulting Architect
2 Chief Inspectors in Manhattan
2 Chief Inspectors in Brooklyn
Chief Inspector in The Bronx, Richmond and Queens
Secretary to the Superintendent

CITY RECORD, BOARD OF

Supervisor of the *City Record*

CHARITIES, DEPARTMENT OF PUBLIC

Deputy Commissioner
Second Deputy Commissioner
Third Deputy Commissioner
Secretary of the Department
Secretary to the Commissioner
Confidential Stenographer
Confidential Inspector
Secretary to the Second Deputy Commissioner
General Inspector
10 Chaplains
10 Deputy Superintendents of Training School
6 Superintendents of Training School

CIVIL SERVICE COMMISSION, MUNICIPAL

10 Expert Examiners
Secretary to the Commission

CORONERS

Clerk to each Coroner in the Boroughs of Manhattan, Richmond, The Bronx, Brooklyn and Queens

COLLEGE OF THE CITY OF NEW YORK

Assistant Secretary
Secretary to the President

CORRECTION, DEPARTMENT OF

Deputy Commissioner
Secretary of the Department
Secretary to the Commissioner
10 Chaplains

CITY COURT

Clerk
Deputy Clerk
Confidential Stenographer and Typewriter Operator
Clerk's Attendant

CITY MAGISTRATES' COURT, FIRST DIVISION

Chief Clerk
Chief Probation Officer
13 Court Clerks

CITY MAGISTRATES' COURT, SECOND DIVISION

Chief Clerk
Chief Probation Officer
17 Court Clerks

MUNICIPAL COURT

Clerk to each District
Clerk to each Justice
Deputy Clerk to each District
44 Assistant Clerks

COURT OF SPECIAL SESSIONS

Chief Clerk
Clerk of the Court, Manhattan
Deputy Clerk of the Court, Manhattan
Clerk of the Court, The Bronx
Deputy Clerk of the Court, The Bronx
Clerk of the Court, Brooklyn
Deputy Clerk of the Court, Brooklyn
Clerk of the Court, Queens
Clerk of the Court, Richmond
Clerk of the Children's Court, Manhattan
Deputy Clerk of the Children's Court, Manhattan and The Bronx
Clerk of the Children's Court, The Bronx
Deputy Clerk of the Children's Court, The Bronx .
Clerk of the Children's Court, Brooklyn
Deputy Clerk of the Children's Court, Brooklyn
Clerk of the Children's Court, Queens
Clerk of the Children's Court, Richmond
Private Secretary to the Chief Justice
Confidential Clerk to the Chief Justice
Chief Probation Officer
Deputy Chief Probation Officer

COURT HOUSE BOARD

Executive Secretary of the Board
Stenographer of the Board
Secretary to the Chairman of the Board
Consulting Architect
Consulting Engineer

DOCKS AND FERRIES, DEPARTMENT OF

2 Deputy Commissioners
Secretary of the Department
Secretary to the Commissioner
Chief Confidential Inspector
Chief Engineer
Expert Accountant
2 Assistant Confidential Inspectors

EXAMINERS, BOARD OF

Clerk to the Board

EDUCATION, DEPARTMENT OF

Secretary of the Board of Education
Sec etary to the City Superintendent
Supt. of School Buildings
Supt. of School Supplies

ELECTIONS, BOARD OF, OF THE CITY OF NEW YORK

6 Chief Clerks for Board and Borough
6 Deputy Chief Clerks for Board and Borough
2 Secretaries to Commissioners
2 Stenographers to Commissioners
9 Clerks to Board

ESTIMATE AND APPORTIONMENT, BOARD OF

Secretary
Assistant Secretary
Chief Clerk
Director of the Bureau of Contract Supervision
Director of the Bureau of Standards

FINANCE, DEPARTMENT OF

3 Deputy Comptrollers
Assistant Deputy Comptroller
Secretary to the Department
Stenographer to the Comptroller
24 Auditors of Accounts
3 Deputy Auditors of Accounts
19 Examining Inspectors
16 Expert Accountants
Chief Accountant and Bookkeeper
Supervising Statistician and Examiner
City Paymaster
8 Deputy City Paymasters
Chief Stock and Bond Clerk
Security Deposit Clerk
Collector of City Revenues and Superintendent of Markets
Clerk to the Comptroller
Deputy Collector of City Revenues
Deputy Superintendent of Markets
10 Bank Messengers
Messenger in the Paymaster's Office and Auditing Bureau
Collector of Assessments and Arrears
Deputy Collector of Assessments and Arrears in each Borough
Receiver of Taxes
2 Deputy Receivers of Taxes in each Borough
2 Appraisers of Real Estate
29 Cashiers
1 Examiner of Accounts of Institutions
Deputy Chamberlain
Secretary to the Chamberlain
Warrant Clerk in the Office of the Chamberlain
2 Bank Messengers in the Office of the Chamberlain
Examiner of Endorsements and Coupons in the Office of the Chamberlain

FIRE DEPARTMENT

Deputy Commissioner
Deputy Commissioner—Brooklyn and Queens
Secretary of the Department
Secretary to the Commissioner
Secretary to the Deputy Commissioner
Cashier — Manhattan, Richmond and The Bronx
Cashier—Brooklyn and Queens
Confidential Stenographer
Inspector of Combustibles
4 Chaplains
Chief, Bureau of Fire Prevention
Deputy Chief, Bureau of Fire Prevention
Chief Inspector, Bureau of Fire Prevention
3 Special Investigators, Bureau of Fire Prevention

HEALTH DEPARTMENT

Secretary of the Department
Secretary to the President
Stenographer to the President
2 Sanitary Engineers
Chaplain

HUNTER COLLEGE OF THE CITY OF NEW YORK

Secretary to the College
Secretary to the President
Stenographer to the Faculty
Confidential Clerk to the Faculty
Bellringer

LAW DEPARTMENT

75 Assistants to the Corporation Counsel with annual salaries not less than $3,000 each
Secretary to the Corporation Counsel
Stenographer to Corporation Counsel

LICENSES, OFFICE OF THE COMMISSIONER

Deputy Commissioner
Secretary to the Commissioner

MAYOR'S OFFICE

Secretary to the Mayor
Assistant Secretary
Executive Secretary
2 Executive Stenographers
Confidential Stenographer
Chief of the Bureau of Weights and Measures
Confidential Inspector of Weights and Measures
Chief of the Bureau of Licenses
Stenographer—Typewriter to the Chief of the Bureau of Licenses
Confidential Clerk, Bureau of Licenses

PARKS, DEPARTMENT OF

Secretary of the Park Board
Secretary to each Commissioner
Stenographer to the Commissioner for Manhattan and Richmond
Stenographer to the Commissioner, Brooklyn
Stenographer to the Commissioner, Queens
Chief Engineer — Brooklyn and Queens
Superintendent of Parks—Manhattan and Richmond
2 Assistant Superintendents of Parks —The Bronx
Superintendent of Recreation—Manhattan and Richmond
Assistant Superintendent of Parks —Manhattan and Richmond
Landscape Architect
Chief Engineer—Manhattan and Richmond
Chief Engineer—The Bronx
Superintendent of Parks — Brooklyn
Superintendent of Parks — The Bronx
Superintendent of Parks—Queens

PERMANENT CENSUS BOARD OF THE CITY OF NEW YORK

Secretary

PRESIDENT OF THE BOARD OF ALDERMEN, OFFICE OF THE

Chief Examiner
2 Examiners
Stenographer

POLICE DEPARTMENT

4 Deputy Commissioners
Secretary to the Commissioner
Executive Clerk to the Commissioner
Secretary to each Deputy Commissioner
Stenographer to the Commissioner
Complaint Clerk
Property Clerk
Assistant Property Clerk
Auditor of Accounts
Stenographer to each Deputy Commissioner

PUBLIC RECREATION COMMISSION

Secretary

PUBLIC WORKS IN EACH BOROUGH, BUREAU OF

Commissioner of Public Works
Assistant Commissioner of Public Works
Secretary to the Commissioner of Public Works
Superintendent of Highways, except Manhattan
Superintendent of Sewers, except Manhattan
Cashier, Bureau of Highways
Superintendent of Public Buildings and Offices
Stenographer to the Commissioner of Public Works, Manhattan
Superintendent of Street Cleaning in Queens and in Richmond
Consulting Engineer, Manhattan
Consulting Engineer, Richmond
Consulting Engineer, Queens
Consulting Engineer of Sewers, Manhattan
Chief Engineer of Sewers, Manhattan
Chief Engineer of Highways, Manhattan
Consulting Engineer, Bronx

SINKING FUND COMMISSION

Clerk of the Commission

STREET CLEANING, DEPARTMENT OF

4 Deputy Commissioners
Confidential Inspector
Secretary to the Commissioner

TAXES AND ASSESSMENTS, DEPARTMENT OF

Assistant to each Commissioner
Secretary to the President
Confidential Stenographer
Secretary to the Board
Chief Clerk in each Borough, except Manhattan

TENEMENT HOUSE DEPARTMENT

2 Deputy Commissioners
3 Superintendents
Secretary of the Department
Secretary to the Commissioner
Secretary to the First Deputy Commissioner
Secretary to the Superintendent—The Bronx
Assistant Superintendent — The Bronx
Stenographer to each Deputy Commissioner
3 Chief Inspectors

WATER SUPPLY OF THE CITY OF NEW YORK, BOARD OF

Chief Engineer
Deputy Chief Engineer
6 Consulting Engineers
16 Division Engineers
6 Department Engineers
Examiner of Real Estate, Taxes and Legislation
6 Designing Engineers
Secretary
2 Assistant Secretaries
Chief Clerk
Auditor
Confidential Secretary to each Commissioner
Private Secretary to Chief Engineer
Superintendent, Board of Water Supply Police

WATER SUPPLY, GAS AND ELECTRICITY, DEPARTMENT OF

Deputy Commissioner in each Borough
Secretary of the Department
Secretary to the Commissioner
Secretary to the Deputy Commissioner, Borough of Manhattan
Secretary to the Deputy Commissioner, Borough of Brooklyn
Stenographer to the Commissioner
Stenographer to the Deputy Commissioner, Borough of Brooklyn
Water Register—Manhattan
Water Register—Brooklyn
Auditor of Accounts
Chief Engineer
Consulting Engineer
Water Register—The Bronx
Chief Engineer of Water Supply
Deputy Chief Engineer
Chief Engineer of Light and Power
Consulting Engineer of Water Supply
Consulting Engineer in the Electrical Bureau
Cashier in each Borough
4 Division Engineers
2 General Inspectors.

The classification of any office or position in the Exempt Class, becoming effective through the adoption of these rules at the time of such adoption, shall in no case be deemed to permit a new appointment to such office or position, except where a vacancy exists or may hereafter be created with authority of law; nor shall such classification be deemed to transfer to the competitive class any office or position classified prior to the adoption of this rule as exempt.

THE COMPETITIVE CLASS

PART I.—UNGRADED POSITIONS

Group 1—Laboratory Positions:

Apothecary
Bacteriologist
Chemist
Laboratory Assistant
Laboratory Supervisor
Pathologist
Assistant Director, Bacteriological Laboratory
Pharmacist

Group 2—Hospital and Asylum Positions, Lay:

Matron
Nurse
Orderly
Supervising Nurse
Steward
Deputy Superintendent
Superintendent
Nurse's Assistant

Group 3—Positions of a Special or Miscellaneous Character:

Arboriculturist
Assistant Fire Marshal
Attendance Officer
Automobile Engineman
Bookbinder
Foreman Bookbinder
Cable Tester
Cataloguer
Curator
Assistant Curator
Chief of Bertillon System
Court Attendant
Custodian
Deputy Commissioner of Taxes and Assessments
Deputy Supervisor of the City Record
Deputy Superintendent of School Supplies
Dietitian
Disinfector
Dockmaster
Electrician
Elevator Despatcher
Estimator
Examiners—
- Chief Examiner, Civil Service Commission
- Civil Service Examiner
- Chief Examiner, Bureau of Fire Prevention
- Examiner, Bureau of Fire Prevention
- Examiner, Board of Education
- Examiner, Board of City Record
- Examiner of Charitable Institutions
- Examiner of Sewer Claims
- Examiner, Law Department

Engineers—
- Asphalt Steam Roller Engineer
- Dynamo Engineer
- Janitor-Engineer
- Marine Engineer
- Pile Driving Engineer
- Stationary Engineer

Stationary Engineer, Electric Pumping Stations
Supervisory Engineer
Engineering Chemist
Fire Marshal
Fuel Engineering Chemist
Gardener
Guard
Head Gardener
Hydrographer
Inspector on Aqueduct
Instructor in Carpentry and Woodworking
Instructor, Gymnasium
Instrument Maker
Interpreter
Investigator
Keeper on Aqueduct
Keeper of Menagerie
Director of Menagerie
Keeper of Morgue
Librarian
Matron, Police or Prison Service
Measurer
Patrolman on Aqueduct
Photographer
Pilot
Principal Coal Sampler
Prison Orderly
Probation Officer
Purchasing Agent
Salary and Grade Examiner
Sealer of Weights and Measures
Searcher
Sergeant on Aqueduct
Steward
Storekeeper
Storekeeper's Helper
Superintendent—
- (1) Bureau of Dependent Adults, Department of Public Charities
- (2) Hospital Supplies
- (3) Laundries
- (4) Municipal Sanatorium, Otisville, N. Y.

Supervisor—
- (1) Complaints
- (2) Janitors

Assistant Supervisor of Janitors
Teacher
Telegraph Operator
Temporary Clerk
Timekeeper
Veterinarian
Visitor, Dept. of Public Charities

Part II.—The Clerical Service.

Group 1—*Clerks:*

Clerk
Financial Clerk
Cashier
Chief Clerk
Assistant Secretary
Ticket Agent
Hospital Clerk

Group 2—*Accountants:*

Accountant
Bookkeeper
Examiner
Chief Accountant or Bookkeeper
Auditor

Group 3—*Stenographers:*

Typewriting Copyist
Book Typewriter
Stenographer and Typewriter
Court Stenographer
Typewriter Accountant

Group 4—*Statisticians:*

Statistical Clerk
Statistician
Tabulator
Assistant Registrar of Records
Registrar of Records
Computer of Assessments

The positions in the Clerical Service are graded according to the amount of the annual compensation, or its equivalent, attaching to each, as follows:

Grade 1— $300 annually
" 2— 600 annually
" 3— 1,200 annually
Grade 4—$1,800 annually
" 5— 2,400 annually, or over

Part III.—The Engineering Service.

Class 1—*Civil:*

The Office Staff—
Grade 1—Junior Topographical Draftsman
" 2—Topographical Draftsman
The Field Staff——
Grade 1—Axeman
Heliotroper
" 2—Rodman
Grade 3—Transitman and Computer
Engineer Inspector
Grade 4—Assistant Engineer
Assistant Topographical
Assistant Surveyor
" 5—Engineer
Surveyor
" 6—Deputy Chief Engineer
Chief Engineer

Class 2—*Architectural:*

Grade 1—Junior Draftsman
Grade 2—Architectural Draftsman
Structural Steel Draftsman
" 3—Chief Draftsman
Architectural Designer
Plan Examiner
Grade 4—Engineer-Inspector
Structural Engineer
Deputy Superintendent of School Buildings
Architect
Chief Plan Examiner

Class 3—*Mechanical:*

Grade 1—Junior Draftsman
" 2—Mechanical Draftsman
Grade 3—Chief Draftsman
" 4—Mechanical Engineer

Class 4—*Electrical:*

Grade 1—Junior Draftsman
" 2—Mechanical Draftsman
Grade 3—Chief Draftsman
" 4—Electrical Engineer

The positions in the Engineering Service are graded according to the amount of the annual compensation, or its equivalent, attaching to each, as follows:

Grade A— $300 annually
" B— 600 annually
" C— 1,200 annually
Grade D—$1,800 annually
" E— 2,400 annually, or over

Part IV.—The Inspection Service.

Group 1—*Inspectors of Public Works:*

Inspector of—
- Boilers
- Cement Tests
- Complaints
- Construction and Repairs
- Dam Construction
- Dock and Pier Construction
- Dredging
- Hydrants, Stopcocks and Shop Work
- Incumbrances
- Iron and Steel Construction
- Masonry Construction

Inspector of—
- Meters and Water Consumption
- Pipe Laying
- Pipes and Castings
- Regulating, Grading and Paving
- Sewer Connections
- Sewer Construction
- Street Openings
- Taps and Connections

Chief Inspector
General Inspector
Superintendent
Assistant Superintendent

Group 2—*Inspectors of Buildings or Building Conditions:*

Inspector of—
- Boiler and Pipe Covering
- Carpentry and Masonry
- Elevators
- Heating and Ventilation
- Iron and Steel Construction
- Masonry Construction
- Painting
- Plastering
- Plumbing

Inspector of—
- Repairs
- Supplies and Repairs

Tenements
Chief Inspector
General Inspector
Lay Sanitary Inspector
Supervising Lay Sanitary Inspector
Supervising Inspector of Tenements

Group 3—Inspectors of Electrical Installations and Conditions:

Inspector of—
- Electrical Conductors
- Light and Power

Chief Inspector
General Inspector

Group 4—Positions of Foreman:

Assistant Foreman
Foreman
General Foreman

Group 5—Inspectors, Miscellaneous:

Inspector of—
- Board of Water Supply
- Boilers, Police Department
- Bookbinding
- Combustibles
- Assistant Inspector of Combustibles
- Complaints
- Dancing Academies
- Fire Alarm Boxes
- Fire Prevention
- Supervisory Inspector of Fire Prevention
- Electrical Inspector
- Foods
- Fuel
- Furniture
- Gas
- Lamps and Gas
- Licenses
- Printing
- Stationery
- Taxicabs
- Transit

Weights and Measures
Supervising Inspector of Weights and Measures
Deputy Chief Inspector of Licenses
Supervising Inspector of Licenses
Master Mechanic
Superintendent of Docks
Assistant Superintendent of Docks
Superintendent of—
- Baths and Comfort Stations
- Repairs and Supplies

Assistant Superintendent of Parks
Chief Inspector
Deputy Chief Inspector
Assistant Chief Inspector

The positions in the Inspection Service are graded according to the amount of annual compensation or to its hourly, daily or weekly equivalent, upon a basis of three hundred working days per annum, attaching to each, as follows:

Grade 1— $900 annually
" 2— 1,200 annually
" 3— 1,800 annually
Grade 4—$2,400 annually
" 5— 3,000 annually, or over

Part V.—The Legal Service.

Assistant Court Clerk
Deputy Assistant Corporation Counsel
Deputy Court Clerk
Examiner with knowledge of Yiddish
Examiner with knowledge of Italian
Junior Assistant Corporation Counsel
Law Clerk
Law Examiner
Librarian, City Court

The positions under the above titles are graded according to the amount of the annual compensation, or its equivalent attaching to each, as follows:

Grade 1— $900 annually
" 2— 1,500 annually
Grade 3—$2,250 annually
" 4— 3,000 annually, or over

Part VI.—The Attendance Service.

Attendant, Gymnasium
Attendant, Playground
Attendant, School Farm
Attendant, for temporary or season service
Attendant, for permanent service
Bridge Keeper
Bridge Tender
Janitor (except Janitor-Engineer)
Janitor, Steam Heating
Messenger
Notice Server
Process Server
Telephone Switchboard Operator
Ticket Chopper
Watchman

The positions in the Attendance Service are graded according to the amount of the annual compensation, or its hourly, daily or weekly equivalent upon a basis of three hundred working days per annum, attaching to each, as follows:

Grade 1— $600 annually
" 2— 1,200 annually
Grade 3—$1,800 annually, or over

Part VII.—The Police Service.

Grade 1—Patrolman (of the first grade, as defined by section 299 of the City Charter)
Grade 2—Sergeant
" 3—Lieutenant
" 4—Captain

Part VIII.—The Fire Service.

Grade 1—Fireman (of the first grade, as defined by section 740 of the City Charter)
Engineer of Steamer
Pilot
" 2—Lieutenant
" 3—Captain
" 4—Battalion Chief
Chief of Construction and Repairs
Grade 4—Chief Inspector
" 5—Deputy Chief
Deputy Chief of Department in Charge of the Borough of Brooklyn and Queens
Deputy Chief in Charge of the Marine Division
" 6—Chief

Part IX.—The Prison Service.

Grade 1—Keeper
" 2—Head Keeper
Grade 3—Warden

Part X.—The Street Cleaning Service.

Grade 1—Assistant Stable Foreman
Assistant Dump Inspector
Assistant Foreman second grade
" 2—Section Foreman
Stable Foreman
Dump Inspector
Time Collector

Grade 3—Assistant Superintendent of Final Disposition
Superintendent of Final Disposition
Master Mechanic
District Superintendent
" 4—Assistant Superintendent
" 5—Superintendent

Part XI.—The Ferry Service.

Class 1:

Grade 1—Mate
" 2—Quartermaster
" 3—Captain

Grade 4—Assistant Superintendent of Ferries
" 5—Superintendent of Ferries

Class 2:

Grade 1—Marine Engineer
" 2—Chief Marine Engineer

Grade 3—Supervising Marine Engineer

Part XII.—The Medical Service.

Assistant Alienist
Resident Alienist
Dentist
Examiner in Lunacy
Medical Clerk
Medical Examiner
Medical Inspector
Medical Officer
Chief Medical Officer
General Medical Officer
Oculist

Physician
Resident Physician
Coroner's Physician
Police Surgeon
Deputy Medical Superintendent
Medical Superintendent
General Medical Superintendent
Sanitary Superintendent
Assistant Sanitary Superintendent

The positions under the above titles are graded according to the amount of the annual compensation, or its equivalent, attaching to each, as follows:

Grade 1— $600 annually
" 2— 1,200 annually
" 3— 1,800 annually

Grade 4—$2,400 annually
" 5— 3,000 annually, or over

THE NON-COMPETITIVE CLASS

Positions in the Department of Public Charities, at compensations not exceeding the amounts set forth below:

Without Maintenance.

	Per Annum.		Per Annum.
Dentist	$400.00	Superintendent of Rendering Plant	$900.00
Hospital Helper	720.00	Watchman	600.00
Hospital Physician at Farm Colony	500.00		
Special Officer (not more than one (1) incumbent)	960.00		

With Maintenance.

Automobile or Ambulance Driver	$960.00	Hospital Helper (Mechanic)	$720.00
Attendant	600.00	Hospital Helper	480.00
Auto Engineman (Ambulance)	1,200.00	Interne	480.00
Baker	900.00	Laundryman or Laundress (in charge)	600.00
Bandmaster	720.00	Orthopedic Mechanic, (one (1) incumbent), $5 per diem	....
Broom Maker Instructor	720.00	Pupil Nurse	180.00
Butcher	720.00	Pupil Examiner	480.00
Cook	900.00	Special Officer (not more than four (4) incumbents)	720.00
Counterman (Head)	720.00	Supervising Nurse	850.00
Deckhand	720.00	Tailor	720.00
Dietitian	900.00	Trained Nurse (Hospital Service)	900.00
Farmer	900.00	Minor employees of whatever designation	150.00
Foreman of Laborers	720.00		
Foreman of Stables	720.00		
Fumigator	600.00		
Housekeeper	900.00		

Positions in the Department of Correction, at compensations not exceeding the amounts set forth below:

Without Maintenance.

	Per Annum.		Per Annum.
Apothecary	$900.00	Deckhand	$720.00
Butcher	1,050.00	Prison Helper	600.00
Cleaner	480.00	Shoemaker	900.00

With Maintenance

Baker	$1,050.00	Hospital Helper-Mechanic	$720.00
Baker, Foreman	1,050.00	Laundress	480.00
Cook (female)	720.00	Orderly	480.00
Cook (male)	900.00	Tailor	720.00
Cutter	1,050.00	Trained Nurse	900.00

SEA VIEW HOSPITAL

With Maintenance.

Morgue Keeper	$720.00	Pharmacist	$720.00
Examining Physician	1,800.00	Resident Physician	1,200.00
Pathologist	1,500.00		

Positions in the Bellevue and Allied Hospitals, at compensations not exceeding the amounts set forth below:

Without Maintenance.

	Per Annum.		Per Annum.
Ambulance Driver	$900.00	Instructors in Anaesthesia	$750.00
Butcher	1,050.00	Medical Bath Attendant	480.00
Employment Agent	900.00	Physician to Out Patients	600.00
Hospital Helper	600.00	Seamstress	720.00
		Watchman	600.00

With Maintenance.

3 Admitting Physicians of 2 years' service in Bellevue Hospital	$1,000.00	Housekeeper, Training School	$900.00
Ambulance Engineman	1,200.00	Laundress	480.00
Assistant Resident Physician (Alcoholic Ward)	600.00	Laundryman	900.00
Barber	480.00	Orderly	480.00
Employment Agent	900.00	Post Graduate Nurse	300.00
Cook (female)	720.00	Pupil Nurse	180.00
Cook (male)	900.00	Resident Obstetrician	1,200.00
Gateman	500.00	Resident Physician, Children's Ward	900.00
Head Pupil Nurse	480.00	Trained Nurse	900.00
Hospital Attendant	480.00	Waiter	480.00
Hospital Helper	420.00	Waitress	480.00
Hospital Helper-Mechanic	720.00	Minor employees of whatever designation	150.00

Positions in the Department of Education, at compensations not exceeding the amounts set forth below:

Manhattan Truant School.

Without Maintenance.

	Per Annum.
Physician	$600.00

With Maintenance.

	Per Annum.		Per Annum.
Caretaker	$720.00	Cook (female)	$720.00
Cleaner	720.00	Cook (male)	900.00

Brooklyn Truant School.

Without Maintenance.

	Per Annum.		Per Annum.
Caretaker	$600.00	Seamstress	$720.00
Gardener—Driver	900.00		

With Maintenance.

Caretaker	$420.00	Laundress	$480.00
Cleaner	480.00	Laundryman	900.00
Cook (female)	720.00	Waitress	480.00
Cook (male)	900.00		

New York Parental School.

Without Maintenance.

	Per Annum.		Per Annum.
Gardener—Driver	$900.00	Physician	$1,000.00

With Maintenance.

Caretaker	$720.00	Laundress	$480.00
Cook (female)	720.00	Laundryman	900.00
Cook (male)	900.00	Waitress	480.00

Positions in the Brooklyn Disciplinary Training School for Boys, at compensation not exceeding the amounts set forth below:

Without Maintenance.

	Per Annum.		Per Annum.
Cleaner	$480.00	Printer	$900.00
Gardener—Driver	900.00	Seamstress	720.00
Hospital Helper	600.00	Shoemaker	900.00
Investigator	900.00	Tailor	900.00
Manual Training Instructor	900.00		

With Maintenance.

Caretaker	$720.00	Laundress	$480.00
Cook	720.00	Orderly	480.00
Hospital Helper	420.00	Stableman	480.00
Housemother	900.00		

Positions in the College of the City of New York, at compensation not exceeding the amounts set forth below:

Without Maintenance.

	Per Annum.
Laboratory Mechanician	$480.00

Positions in the Department of Health, at compensations not exceeding the amounts set forth below:

Hospitals for Contagious Diseases in New York City.

Without Maintenance.

	Per Annum.		Per Annum.
Attending Physician at Tuberculosis Clinics	$600.00	Hospital Clerk, with a knowledge of Italian, Tuberculosis Clinic	$600.00
Butcher	720.00	Librarian	900.00

With Maintenance.

Automobile Engineman (Ambulance)	$900.00	Hospital Physician	$1,800.00
Domestic	960.00	Interne	300.00
Helper	780.00	Nurse	1,200.00
		Orderly	780.00

Tuberculosis Sanatorium, Otisville, N. Y.

Without Maintenance.

	Per Annum.		Per Annum.
Blacksmith	$780.00	Laborer	$1,020.00
Carpenter	936.00	Plumber	900.00
Dairyman	900.00	Stationary Engineer	900.00
Fireman	840.00	Storekeeper	780.00
Laboratory Assistant	600.00	Tinsmith	900.00

With Maintenance.

Domestic	$960.00	Hospital Physician	$2,400.00
Helper	600.00	Nurse	900.00
Hospital Clerk	600.00	Orderly	600.00
		Telephone Switchboard Operator	240.00

Positions in the Municipal Civil Service Commission, at compensation not exceeding the amounts set forth below:

	Per Day.
Monitor	$5.00

Positions in the Department of Docks and Ferries, at compensations not exceeding the amounts set forth below:

Without Maintenance.

	Per Day.		Per Day.
Diver	$10.00	Diver's Tender	$3.50

Positions in the Police Department (Steamer "Patrol"), at compensations not exceeding the amounts set forth below:

Without Maintenance.

	Per Annum.		Per Annum.
Cook	$600.00	Steward	$360.00

Positions in the Board of Inebriety at compensations not exceeding the amounts set forth below:

With Maintenance.

	Per Annum.		Per Annum.
Farmer and Caretaker	$720.00	Helper	$480.00
			Per Day.
Helper			$2.00

Positions in the Department of Street Cleaning, at compensations not exceeding the amounts set forth below:

Without Maintenance.

	Per Day.		Per Day.
Deckhand	$2.00	Fireman	$2.50
			Per Week.
Marine Engineer			$30.00
	Per Day.		Per Day.
Marine Engineer's Assistant	$2.35	Mate	$2.50
Master	3.33		

Position in the Department of Water Supply, Gas and Electricity, at compensations not exceeding the amounts set forth below:

Without Maintenance.	Per Annum.
Lighter of Markets...	**$360.00**

THE LABOR CLASS

PART I.

Cleaner (Women)
Cleaner (Men)
Climber and Pruner
Coal Passer
Driver
Driver, *Dep't Street Cleaning*
Driver, *Street Cleaning Bureau, Offices of the Borough Presidents, Richmond and Queens*
Dump Boardman, *Dep't of Street Cleaning*
Dump Boardman, *Street Cleaning Bureau, Offices of the Borough Presidents, Richmond and Queens*
Hostler
Laborer
Licensed Fireman
Paver
Rammer
Sewer Cleaner
Stableman
Sweeper, *Dep't of Street Cleaning*
Sweeper, *Street Cleaning Bureau, Offices of the Borough Presidents, Richmond and Queens*

PART II.

Asphalt Worker
Batteryman, *Fire Dep't*
Batteryman's Assistant, *Fire Dep't*
Blaster
Bridgeman, *Dep't of Docks and Ferries*
Cabinet Maker
Carriage-body Maker, *Fire Dep't*
Carriage Trimmer
Cement Mason
Climber and Pruner
Clock Repairer
Deckhand
Electrician's Helper
Elevator Constructor's Helper
Elevatorman
Glazier
Hose Repairer, *Fire Dep't*
Lineman
Machinist's Helper
Machine Woodworker
Marine Stoker
Marble Polisher
Marble Setter
Marble Setter's Helper
Mason's Helper
Nickel Plater, *Fire Dep't*
Oiler
Pattern Maker
Rubber-tire Repairer, *Fire Dep't*
Scowman, *Dep't of Street Cleaning*
Ship Caulker
Stone Cutter
Stone Mason
Thermostat Repairer
Water Tender, *Dep't of Docks and Ferries*
Well Driver, *Dep't of Water Supply, Gas and Electricity*
Wheelwright
Wireman
Carriage Painter
Coal Sampler
Upholsterer

PART III.

Automobile Machinist
Blacksmith
Blacksmith's Helper
Boilermaker
Boilermaker's Helper
Brass Finisher, *Fire Dep't*
Bricklayer
Bridge Painter
Bridgeman and Riveter
Cable Splicer, *Fire Dep't*
Carpenter
Compositor
Core Maker, *Fire Dep't*
Decorator
Dock Builder
Feeder
Flagger
Grainer
Harness Maker
Horseshoer (Fireman)
Horseshoer (Floorman)
House Painter
Housesmith
Letterer
Machinist
Marine Sounder, *Dep't of Docks and Ferries*
Moulder, *Fire Dep't*
Pipe Caulker
Plasterer
Plumber
Plumber's Helper
Pressman
Rigger
Sheet Metal Worker
Ship Carpenter
Steam Fitter
Steam Fitter's Helper
Varnisher
Saw Filer
Striper
Tapper

PART IV.

Positions in Hospitals:

Boatman
Carpenter
Deckhand
Driver
Elevatorman
Fireman
Laborer

CHAPTER 7 OF THE CONSOLIDATED LAWS

CIVIL SERVICE LAW

CONSTITUTION OF THE STATE OF NEW YORK.

ARTICLE V.

Civil Service Appointments and Promotions.

§ 9. Appointments and promotions in the civil service of the state, and of all the civil divisions thereof, including cities and villages, shall be made according to merit and fitness, to be ascertained, so far as practicable, by examinations, which, so far as practicable, shall be competitive; provided, however, that honorably discharged soldiers and sailors from the army and navy of the United States in the late civil war, who are citizens and residents of this state, shall be entitled to preference in appointment and promotion, without regard to their standing on any list from which such appointment or promotion may be made. Laws shall be made to provide for the enforcement of this section.

Chap. 15.

An Act in relation to the civil service of the state of New York and the cities and civil divisions thereof, constituting chapter 7 of the Consolidated Laws.

Became a law February 17, 1909.

The People of the State of New York, represented in Senate and Assembly, do enact as follows:

ARTICLE I.

Short Title; Definitions.

Section 1. Short title.—This chapter shall be known as the civil service law.

§ 2. Definitions.—When used in this chapter.

1. The term "Commission" or "State Commission" means the State Civil Service Commission.
2. The term "municipal commission" means the municipal civil service commission of a city.

3. The "civil service" of the state of New York or any of its civil divisions or cities includes all offices and positions of trust or employment in the service of the state or of such civil division or city, except such offices and positions in the militia and the military departments as are or may be created under the provisions of article eleven of the constitution.

4. The "state service" shall include all such offices and positions in the service of the state or of any of its civil divisions except a city.

5. The "city service" shall include such positions in the service of any city.

6. The term "appointing officer" signifies the officer, commission, board or body having the power of appointment to subordinate positions in any office, court, department, commission, board or institution.

§ 3. State Civil Service Commission.—The governor is authorized to appoint, by and with the advice and consent of the senate, three persons, not more than two of whom shall be adherents of the same political party, as civil service commissioners, and said three commissioners shall constitute the state civil service commission. They shall hold no other political place under the state of New York. On or before the first day of May, in the year one thousand nine hundred and thirteen the governor shall designate one member of the present state civil service commission to serve as a member of the commission until the first day of February, one thousand nine hundred and fifteen; one until the first day of February, one thousand nine hundred and seventeen; and one until the first day of February, one thousand nine hundred and nineteen. Upon the expiration of each of said terms, the term of office of each commissioner hereafter appointed shall be six years from the first day of February of the year in which he shall be appointed. Vacancies shall be filled by appointment of the governor for the unexpired term. Each of the three commissioners shall receive a salary of five thousand dollars a year, and each of said commissioners shall be paid his necessary expenses incurred in the discharge of his duties as a commissioner.

§ 4. Officers and employees of the commission.—The commission shall elect one of its members to be president, and may employ a chief examiner, a secretary and such other officers, clerks and examiners as it may deem necessary or proper to carry out the purposes of this chapter, and such employees shall hold office during the pleasure of the commission. The chief examiner shall be entitled to receive a salary at the rate of three thousand six hundred dollars a year, and he shall be paid his necessary traveling expenses incurred in the discharge of his duty. The secretary, and other officers, clerks and examiners shall receive salaries to be fixed by the commission, and the secretary shall also be paid his necessary traveling expenses incurred in the discharge of his duty. The commission may select suitable persons in the official service of the state or any of its civil divisions, after consulting the head of the department or office in which such persons serve, to act as examiners under its direction. Persons so selected shall be entitled to compensation from the commission for their necessary expenses occasioned by the service actually rendered, in addition to the regular service required in the department or office where they are regularly employed. The compensation of examiners shall not exceed five dollars per day, except in case of special and expert examiners employed in the preparation of questions and rating of candidates; the commission shall not expend or authorize the expenditure of moneys for any purpose in excess of the sums appropriated therefor by law.

§ 5. Rooms and accommodations.—It shall be the duty of the trustees of public buildings to cause suitable and convenient rooms and accommodations to be assigned or provided, and to be furnished, heated and lighted, at the capitol in the city of Albany, for carrying on the work and examinations of said commission, and said commission may order the necessary stationery, postage stamps, an official seal and other articles to be supplied, and the necessary printing to be done for its official use. It shall be the duty of the officers of the state of New York or of any civil division thereof, at any place where examinations are directed by the commission or its rules to be held, to allow the reasonable use of public buildings, and to heat and light the same for holding such examinations, and in all proper ways to facilitate the same.

§ 6. The powers and duties of the commission.—The state civil service commission shall

First. Prescribe, amend and enforce suitable rules and regulations for carrying into effect the provisions of this chapter and of section nine of article five of the constitution of the state of New

York, as herein provided. The rules prescribed by the state and municipal commissions pursuant to the provisions of this chapter shall have the force and effect of law.

Second. Keep minutes of its own proceedings and records of its examinations and other official action.

Third. Make investigations concerning and report upon all matters touching the enforcement and effect of the provisions of this chapter and the rules and regulations prescribed thereunder, concerning the action of any examiner or subordinate of the commission and any person in the public service, in respect to the execution of this chapter, and in the course of such investigations each commissioner and the secretary and the chief examiner shall have power to administer oaths.

Fourth. Have power to subpoena and require the attendance in this state of witnesses and the production hereby of books and papers pertinent to the investigation and inquiries hereby authorized and to examine them and such public records as it shall require in relation to any matter which it is required to investigate. And for the purposes of the examination hereby directed, the commission possesses all the powers conferred by the legislative law upon a committee of the legislature or by the code of civil procedure upon a board or committee, and may invoke the power of any court of record in the state to compel the attendance and testifying of witnesses and the production thereby of books and papers as aforesaid.

Fifth. Make an annual report to the governor for transmission to the legislature, showing its own action, the rules and regulations and the exceptions thereto in force, and the practical effects thereof and any suggestions it may approve for the more effectual accomplishment of the purposes of this chapter.

Sixth. Meet in Albany at least once in each calendar month, except the month of August, and hold such other meetings as the needs of the public service may require. A majority of the members of the commission shall constitute a quorum.

§ 7. Attendance of witnesses; fees.—Witnesses and officers to subpoena and secure the attendance of witnesses before said commission shall be entitled to the same fees as are allowed witnesses in civil cases in courts of record. Such fees need not be prepaid, but the comptroller shall draw his warrant for the payment of the amount thereof, when the same shall have been certified to by the president of the commission, and duly proved by affidavit or otherwise to the satisfaction of the said comptroller; and all state, county, town, municipal and other officers and their deputies, clerks, subordinates and employees shall afford the said board all reasonable facilities in conducting the inquiries specified in this chapter, and give inspection to said board of all books, papers and documents belonging, or in any way appertaining to the respective offices, and shall also produce sa'd books and papers and shall attend and testify when required to do so by said commission.

§ 8. Duties of public officers.—It shall be the duty of all officers of the state of New York or of any civil division or city thereof to conform to and comply with and to aid in all proper ways in carrying into effect the provisions of this chapter, and the rules and regulations prescribed thereunder and any modification thereof. No officer or officers having the power of appointment or employment shall select or appoint any person for appointment, employment, promotion or reinstatement except in accordance with the provisions of this chapter and the rules and regulations prescribed thereunder. Any person employed or appointed contrary to the provisions of this chapter or of the rules and regulations established thereunder, shall be paid by the officer or officers so employing or appointing, or attempting to employ or appoint him, the compensation agreed upon for any services performed under such appointment or employment, or in case no compensation is agreed upon, the actual value of such services, and any expenses incurred in connection therewith, and shall have a cause of action against such officer or officers or any of them for such sum or sums and for the costs of the action. No public officer shall be reimbursed by the state or any of its civil divisions for any sums so paid or recovered in any such action.

§ 9. Unclassified service; classified service.—The civil service of the state and of each of its civil divisions and cities shall be divided into the unclassified service and the classified service. The unclassified service shall comprise all elective offices, all offices filled by election or appointment by the legislature on joint ballot; all persons appointed by name in any statute; all legislative officers and employees, all offices filled by appointment by the governor, either upon or without confirmation by the senate, except officers and employees in the executive offices; all election officers, the head or heads of any department of the government, and persons employed in or who seek to enter the public service as superintendents, principals or teachers in a public school or academy or in a state normal school or college. The classified service shall comprise all positions not included in the unclassified service. All appointments or employments in the classified service, except those of veterans of the civil war, honorably discharged from the military or naval service of the United States, shall be for a probationary term not exceeding the time fixed in the rules.

§ 10. Rules for the classified state service.—The commission shall from time to time make rules for the classification of the offices, places and employments in the classified service of the state, and from time to time rules for the classification of the offices, places and employments in such civil divisions thereof, except cities, as after due inquiry by the commission shall be found practicable, and for appointments and promotions therein and examinations therefor, not inconsistent with the constitution and the provisions of this chapter, and shall amend the same from time to time. No examination or registration shall be required of persons to be employed as laborers in the state service. Such rules and any modifications thereof, shall take effect when approved by the governor. Due notice of the contents of such rules, and of any modifications thereof, shall be given by mail to appointing officers and heads of departments affected thereby, and such rules shall be printed for public distribution. Subject to the provisions of this chapter and of the rules established thereunder, the commission shall make regulations for and have control of examinations for the service of the state and the civil divisions thereof, except cities, and shall supervise and preserve the records of the same, but such examinations shall be held at least once a year in each of the following places: Albany, Amsterdam, Auburn, Binghamton, Buffalo, Dunkirk, Elmira, Geneva, Hornell, Ithaca, Jamestown, Johnstown, Kingston, Lockport, Malone, Middletown, Newburg, New York, Ogdensburg, Olean, Oneonta, Oswego, Plattsburg, Poughkeepsie, Rochester, Saratoga, Syracuse, Utica and Watertown; and shall cover in each place all offices and positions for which competitive examinations are required, except such examinations as require special tools, machinery, appliances or laboratory facilities.

§ 11. The classified city service.—The mayor of each city in this state shall appoint and employ suitable persons to prescribe, amend and enforce rules for the classification of the offices, places and employments in the classified service of such city, and for appointments and promotions therein and examinations therefor; and for the registration and selection of laborers for employment therein, not inconsistent with the constitution and the provisions of this chapter, and shall amend the same from time to time. Such persons shall be municipal civil service commissioners and shall constitute the municipal civil service commission of such city. All appointments or designations of municipal civil service commissioners shall be made in such manner that not more than two-thirds of such commissioners in any city shall at any time be adherents of the same political party. Such rules herein prescribed and established, and all regulations now existing for appointment and promotion in the civil service of said city, and any subsequent modification thereof, whether prescribed under the authority of a general law or of any special or local law, shall be valid and take or continue in effect only upon the approval of the mayor of the city and of the state civil service commission. The authority by this section conferred shall not be so exercised as to take from any policeman or fireman any right or benefit conferred by law, or existing under any lawful regulation of the department in which he serves. All examinations herein authorized shall be public, and all rules shall be published, and, with all the proceedings and papers connected with said examinations, shall be at all times subject to the inspection of said state commission and its agents; and said commission shall set forth in its report the character and practical effects of such examinations, together with its views as to the improvement and extension of the same, and also copies of all rules made under the authority hereby conferred. Subject to the provisions of this chapter and of said rules, the municipal commission of any city shall make regulations for and have control of examinations and registrations for the service of such city, and shall supervise and preserve the records of the same. In case for any reason, the mayor of any city within sixty days after he has the power to appoint, fails to appoint such municipal commissioners, the state commission shall appoint them to hold office until the expiration of the term of the mayor then in office and until their successors are appointed and qualify. It shall be the duty of such persons to prepare and to procure the approval of the rules herein provided for, and, if they fail to do so within sixty days after their appointment, the state commission shall forthwith make said rules. It shall be the duty of such persons to make reports from time to time to the state commission, whenever said commission may request, of the manner in which this law, and the rules and regulations thereunder, have been and are administered, and the results of their administration in such city, and of such other matters as said commission may require, and annually on or before the fifteenth day of January, to make such a report to said commission; and it shall be the duty of said state commission in its annual report to set out either these reports, or a sufficient abstract or summary thereof, to give full and clear information as to their contents. A copy of the roster of the classified civil service of such city shall be transmitted to the state commission with the annual report aforesaid, and shall be filed in the office of said commission as a public record. The mayor may at any time remove any municipal civil service commissioner appointed by him. Said state commission may also, by unanimous vote of the three commissioners, with the written approval of the governor, remove any municipal civil service commissioner appointed or employed under the authority of this section, for incompetency, inefficiency, neglect of duty or violation of the provisions of this chapter, or of the rules and regulations in force thereunder, or of any of them, specifying in writing the particulars of the incompetency, inefficiency, neglect of duty or violation charged, and filing the same as a public document in the office of the city clerk, or if there be no city clerk, in the office of the clerk of the board of aldermen, and a certified transcript thereof in the office of the state civil service commission, first giving such commissioner an opportunity to make a personal explanation in self-defense. Whenever a municipal civil service commissioner has been removed by the unanimous vote of the three state commissioners, with the written approval of the governor, or whenever any municipal commissioner shall resign or be removed by the mayor pending an investigation by the state commission of the administration of the civil service of the city in which such person is a municipal commissioner, or whenever any municipal commissioner shall resign or be removed by the mayor pending a hearing by the state commission of charges preferred against such municipal commissioner, the state commission and not the mayor of such city shall have power to appoint persons to fill such vacancies, and such persons so appointed by the state commission shall hold office as municipal civil service commissioners of such city until the expiration of the term of the mayor then in office and until their successors are appointed and qualify. Said state commission may at any time, by unanimous vote of the three commissioners, amend or rescind any rule, regulation or classification prescribed under provisions of this section, provided that said state commission shall state the reasons for such action in writing, and file the same and a certified transcript thereof as a public document as hereinbefore provided, and give an opportunity to the municipal civil service commissioners concerned to make a personal explanation and to file papers in opposition to such action. The said state commission, however, shall not take such action upon any ground other than that the provisions or purposes of this chapter are not properly or sufficiently carried out by such rule, regulation or classification, nor without specifying in writing and detail in what particular such provisions or purposes are not carried out, nor shall said state commission exempt from competitive examination any position or place or employment in any city without the consent of the municipal commission of such city.

§ 12. Classification.—The offices and positions in the classified service of the state or of any civil division or city thereof for which civil service rules shall be established pursuant to this chapter, shall be arranged in four classes to be designated as the exempt class, the competitive class, the non-competitive class and, in cities, the labor class.

§ 13. The exempt class.—The following positions shall be included in the exempt class:

1. The deputies of principal executive officers authorized by law to act generally for and in place of their principals;

2. One secretary of each officer, board and commission, authorized by law to appoint a secretary;

3. One clerk, and one deputy clerk if authorized by law, of each court, and one clerk of each elective judicial officer;

4. In the state service, all unskilled laborers and such skilled laborers as are not included in the competitive class or the non-competitive class; and in addition thereto there may be included in the exempt class all other subordinate offices for the filling of which competitive or non-competitive examination may be found to be not practicable. But no office or position shall be deemed to be in the exempt class unless it is specifically named in such class

in the rules, and the reasons for each such exemption shall be stated separately in the annual reports of the commission. Not more than one appointment shall be made to or under the title of any such office or position, unless a different number is specifically mentioned in such rules. Appointments to positions in the exempt class may be made without examination.

§ 14. The competitive class.—The competitive class shall include all positions for which it is practicable to determine the merit and fitness of applicants by competitive examination, and shall include all positions now existing, or hereafter created, of whatever functions, designations or compensation, in each and every branch of the classified service, except such positions as are in the exempt class, the non-competitive class or the labor class. Appointments shall be made to or employment shall be given in all positions in the competitive class that are not filled by promotion, reinstatement, transfer or reduction under the provisions of this chapter, and the rules in pursuance thereof, by appointment from among those graded highest in open competitive examinations conducted by the state or municipal commission, except as herein otherwise provided. The term of eligibility shall be fixed for each eligible list at not less than one nor more than four years. Appointment shall be made from the eligible list most nearly appropriate for the group in which the position to be filled is classified, and a new list shall be created for a stated position or group of positions only when there is no appropriate list existing from which appointment may be made. No person shall be appointed or employed under any title not appropriate to the duties to be performed, and no person shall be transferred to, or assigned to perform the duties of, any position subject to competitive examination, unless he shall have previously passed an open competitive examination equivalent to that required for such position, or unless he shall have served with fidelity for at least three years in a similar position. Appointments to positions in the state service, the duties of which are confined to a locality outside of Albany county, shall, so far as practicable, be made from residents of the judicial district including such locality. The examinations shall be public and shall be practical in their character and shall relate to those matters which will fairly test the relative capacity and fitness of the persons examined to discharge the duties of that service into which they seek to be appointed. Such commissions shall prepare lists of preliminary requirements and subjects of examination for the several positions or groups of positions in the competitive class and shall publish their rules and such information, and advertise such examinations in such manner as the nature of the examinations may require. Each of such commissions shall require intending competitors to file in its office a reasonable length of time before the date of any examination, a formal application in which the applicant shall state under oath:

1. His full name, residence and post-office address.
2. His age and the place and date of his birth.
3. His health and physical capacity for the public service.
4. His right of preference by reason of military or naval service.
5. His business or employment, and residence for at least the previous five years.
6. Such other information as may reasonably be required touching the applicant's merit and fitness for the public service.

Blank forms for such applications shall be furnished by said commissions without charge to all persons requesting the same. Such commissions may require in connection with such application such certificates of citizens, physicians, public officers or others having knowledge of the applicant, as the good of the service may require. Such commissions may refuse to examine an applicant, or after examination to certify an eligible, who is found to lack any of the established preliminary requirements for the examination or position for which he applies; or who is physically so disabled as to be rendered unfit for his performance of the duties of the position to which he seeks appointment; or who is addicted to the habitual use of intoxicating beverages to excess; or who has been guilty of a crime or of infamous or notoriously disgraceful conduct; or who has been dismissed from the public service for delinquency or misconduct; or who has intentionally made a false statement of any material fact, or practiced, or attempted to practice, any deception or fraud in his application, in his examination, or in securing his eligibility or appointment. When the position to be filled involves fiduciary responsibility, the appointing officer, where permitted by law, may require the appointee to furnish a bond or other security and shall notify the state or municipal commission of the amount and necessary details thereof.

§ 15. Exemptions from competitive examination.—Positions in the competitive class may be filled without examination as follows:

1. Whenever there are urgent reasons for filling a vacancy in the competitive class and there is no list of persons eligible for appointment after competitive examination, the appointing officer may nominate a person to the state or municipal commission for non-competitive examination, and if such nominee shall be certified by such commission as qualified after such non-competitive examination, he may be appointed provisionally to fill such vacancy until a selection and appointment can be made after competitive examination, but such provisional appointment shall not continue for a longer period than two months, nor shall successive temporary appointments be made to the same position under this subdivision.

2. In case of a vacancy in a position in the competitive class where peculiar and exceptional qualifications of a scientific, professional or educational character are required, and upon satisfactory evidence that for specified reasons competition in such special case is impracticable and that the position can be best filled by the selection of some designated person of high and recognized attainments in such qualities, the state or municipal commission may suspend the provisions of the rule requiring competition in such case, but no such suspension shall be general in its application to such place, and all such cases of suspension shall be reported in the annual reports of such commissions with the reasons for the same.

3. When the services to be rendered by an appointee in the state service are for a temporary period not to exceed one month and the need of such service is important and urgent, the appointing officer may select for such temporary service any person on the proper list of those eligible for a permanent appointment without regard to his standing on such list.

§ 16. Promotions; transfer; reinstatement; reduction.—Vacancies in positions in the competitive class shall be filled, so far as practicable, by promotion from among persons holding positions in a lower grade in the department, office or institution in which the vacancy exists. Promotion shall be based upon merit and competition and upon the superior qualifications of the person promoted as shown by his previous service, due weight being given to seniority. For the purposes of this section an increase in the salary or other compensation of any person holding an office or position within the scope of the rules in forces hereunder beyond the limit fixed for the grade in which such office or position is classified, shall be deemed a promotion. No promotion, transfer or reinstatement shall be made from a position in one class to a position in another class unless the same be specially authorized by the state or municipal commission, nor shall a person be promoted or transferred to a position for original entrance to which there is required by this chapter or the rules an examination involving essential tests or qualifications different from or higher than those required for original entrance to the position held by such person, unless he shall have passed the examination or attained a place upon the eligible list for such higher position.

§ 17. The non-competitive class.—The non-competitive class shall include such positions as are not in the exempt class or the labor class and which it is impracticable to include in the competitive class. Appointments to positions in the non-competitive class shall be made after such non-competitive examination as is prescribed by the rules.

§ 18. The labor class in cities.—The labor class in cities shall include unskilled laborers and such skilled laborers as are not included in the competitive class or the non-competitive class. Vacancies in the labor class in cities shall be filled by appointment from lists of applicants registered by the municipal commissions. Preference in employment from such lists shall be given according to date of application. There shall be separate lists of applicants for different kinds of labor or employment, and the commissions may establish separate labor lists for various institutions and departments. Where the labor service of any department or institution extends to separate localities, the commissions may provide separate registration lists for each district or locality. The commissions shall require an applicant for registration for the labor service to furnish such evidence or pass such examination as they may deem proper with respect to his age, residence, physical condition, ability to labor, skill, capacity and experience in the trade or employment for which he applies.

§ 19. Official roster; reports of appointing officers.—No person shall be appointed to or employed in any position in the classified service of the state or of any civil division or city thereof for which rules have been prescribed pursuant to the provisions of this chapter, until he has passed an examination or is shown to be especially exempted from such examination in conformity with such rules and the provisions of this chapter. It shall be the duty of each appointing officer of the state or any such civil division thereof, except cities, to report to the state civil service commission forthwith upon such appointment or employment the name of such appointee or employee, the title and character of his office or employment, the date of the commencement of service by virtue thereof and the salary or compensation thereof, and to report from time to time and upon the date of official action in or knowledge of each case, any separation of a person from the service, or other change therein, and such other information as the commission may require, in order to keep the roster hereinafter mentioned. The commission shall keep in its office an official roster of the classified civil service of the state and of each of the civil divisions thereof for which rules have been prescribed pursuant to this chapter, except cities, and shall enter thereon the name of each and every person who has been appointed to, employed, promoted or reinstated in any position in such service, upon such evidence as it may require or deem satisfactory that such person was appointed to, promoted or reinstated in the service in conformity with the provisions of law and the rules prescribed pursuant to this chapter. The official roster shall show opposite or in connection with each name the date of appointment, employment, promotion or reinstatement, the compensation of the position, the date of commencement of service, and date of transfer in or separation from service by dismissal, resignation, cancellation of appointment or death. In like manner the municipal commission of each city shall keep in its office an official roster of the classified civil service of such city, and shall enter thereon the name of each and every person who has been appointed to, employed, promoted or reinstated in any position in such service, upon such evidence as it may require or deem satisfactory that such person was appointed to, or employed, promoted or reinstated in the service in conformity with the provisions of law and of the rules, and it shall be the duty of each appointing officer of such city to report to such municipal commission in like manner as is hereinbefore provided for reports from appointing officers to the state commission.

§ 20. Disbursing officers.—It shall be unlawful for the comptroller or other fiscal officer of the state or any civil division or city thereof for which civil service rules have been prescribed pursuant to this chapter, to draw, sign or issue, or authorize the drawing, signing or issuing of any warrant on the treasurer or other disbursing officer of the state or such civil division or city thereof, for the payment of, or for the treasurer or other disbursing officer of the state or of such civil division or city thereof, to pay any salary or compensation to any officer, clerk or other person in the classified service of the state or of such civil division or city thereof, unless an estimate, payroll or account for such salary or compensation, containing the names of the persons to be paid, shall bear the certificate of the state civil service commission, or in the case of the service of a city, the certificate of the municipal civil service commission of such city, that the persons named in such estimate, payroll or account have been appointed or employed or promoted in pursuance of law and of the rules made in pursuance of law. Any officer, clerk or other person entitled to be certified by said commission, or either of them, to the comptroller, treasurer or other fiscal or disbursing officer of the state or any city or civil division thereof, as having been appointed or employed in pursuance of law and of the rules made in pursuance of law and refused such certificate, may maintain a proceeding by mandamus to compel such commission or commissions to issue such certificate. If the state civil service commission or any municipal civil service commission shall find that any person has been transferred, assigned to perform duties or reinstated in violation of any provision of the civil service law or of the rules adopted thereunder, it shall so notify the comptroller or other fiscal officer of the state or of the appropriate civil division or city thereof and thereafter such officer shall not draw, sign or issue or authorize the drawing, signing or issuing of any warrant on the treasurer or other disbursing officer for the payment of salary or compensation to any such person. Any such person may maintain a proceeding by mandamus to compel the payment of salary or compensation so withheld, if lawfully entitled thereto. Any sums paid contrary to the provisions of this section may be recovered from any officer or officers making such appointment in contravention of the provisions of law and of the rules made in pursuance of law, or any officer signing or countersigning or authorizing the signing or countersigning of any warrant for the payment of the same, and from the sureties on his official bond, in an action in the supreme court of the state, maintained by a citizen resident therein, who is assessed for and is liable to pay, or within one year before the commencement of the action, has paid a tax therein. All moneys recovered in any action brought under the provisions of this section must, when collected, be paid into the treasury of the state or such civil division thereof except that the plaintiff in any such action shall be entitled to receive for his own use the taxable costs of such action.

§ 21. Preferences allowed honorably discharged soldiers, sailors and marines.—In every public department and upon all public works of the state of New York and of the cities, counties, towns and villages thereof, honorably discharged soldiers, sailors and marines from the army and navy of the United States in the late civil war who are citizens and residents of this state, shall be entitled to preference in appointment and promotion without regard to their standing on any list from which such appointment or promotion may be made to all competitive and non-competitive positions provided their qualifications and fitness shall have been ascertained as provided in this chapter and the rules and regulations in pursuance thereof; and a person thus preferred shall not be disqualified from holding any position in the civil service on account of his age or by reason of any physical disability, provided such age or disability does not render him incompetent to perform the duties of the position applied for. Whenever any list of eligible persons, prepared under authority of this chapter, shall contain the names of honorably discharged soldiers, sailors and marines entitled to preference as aforesaid, any reference in this chapter or in the rules and regulations in pursuance thereof to the persons standing highest on such list shall be deemed to indicate those standing highest of those entitled to preference by the provisions of this section and such person shall be given preference on any list of registered applicants for employment in the labor service, in accordance with the dates of their several applications as though such applications had been filed prior to those of any persons on such lists not entitled to the preference provided by this section. A refusal to allow the preference provided for in this and the next succeeding section to any honorably discharged soldier, sailor or marine or a reduction of his compensation intended to bring about his resignation shall be deemed a misdemeanor, and such honorably discharged soldier, sailor or marine shall have a right of action therefor in any court of competent jurisdiction for damages, and also a remedy by mandamus for righting the wrong.

§ 22. Power of removal limited.—Every person whose rights may be in any way prejudiced contrary to any of the provisions of this section shall be entitled to a writ of mandamus to remedy the wrong. No person holding a position by appointment or employment in the state of New York or in the several cities, counties, towns or villages thereof who is an honorably discharged soldier, sailor or marine, having served as such in the Union army or navy during the war of the rebellion, or who is an honorably discharged soldier, sailor or marine, having served as such in the volunteer army or navy of the United States during the Spanish war or who shall have served the term required by law in the volunteer fire department of any city, town or village in the state, or who shall have been a member thereof at the time of the disbandment of such volunteer fire department shall be removed from such position except for incompetency or misconduct shown after a hearing upon due notice upon stated charges, and with the right to such employee or appointee to a review by a writ of certiorari. If the position so held by any such honorably discharged soldier, sailor or marine or volunteer fireman shall become unnecessary or be abolished for reasons of economy or otherwise, the said honorably discharged soldier, sailor or marine or volunteer fireman holding the same shall not be discharged from the public service, but shall be transferred to any branch of the said service for duty in such position as he may be fitted to fill, receiving the same compensation therefor, and it is hereby made the duty of all persons clothed with power of appointment to make such transfer effective. The burden of proving incompetency or misconduct shall be upon the person alleging the same. In every county of the state wholly included within the limits of a city but not comprising the whole of such city, no regular clerk or head of a bureau or person holding a position in the classified state civil service, subject to competitive examination, shall be removed until he has been allowed an opportunity of making an explanation; and in every case of a removal the true grounds thereof shall be forthwith entered upon the records of the department of the office in which he has been employed, and a copy filed with the state civil service commission. In case of a removal, a statement showing the reasons therefor shall be filed in the department or office where such clerk, head of a bureau or person had been employed. Whenever such offices, positions or employments in every county of the state hereinbefore specified are abolished or made unnecessary, it shall be the duty of the head of the department or office in which such persons had been employed, to furnish the names of the person or persons affected to the state civil service commission, with a statement in the case of each of the date of his original appointment in the service. It shall be the duty of the state civil service commission forthwith to place the names of said persons upon a list of suspended employees for the office or position or for the class of work in which they have been employed, or for any corresponding or similar office, position or class of work, and to certify the said persons for reinstatement or re-employment in the order of their original appointment before making certification from any other list. The failure of any person on any such list for reinstatement or re-employment to accept after reasonable notice, an office or position in the same county and at the same salary or wages as the position formerly held by him, shall be held to be a relinquishment of his right to reinstatement as herein stated. Nothing in this section shall be construed to apply to the position of private secretary, cashier or deputy of any official or department.

§ 23. Compensation of veterans reinstated by order of the courts.—Any honorably discharged soldier, sailor or marine, who having served as such in the union army or navy during the war of the rebellion, shall have been, or may hereafter be removed from any position held by him by appointment or employment in the state of New York or in the several cities, counties, towns or villages thereof in contravention or violation of any provision of section 22 of this article and who shall have been restored to such position or employment either by a peremptory writ of mandamus of the supreme court or by final order on a writ of certiorari, as authorized by said section 22, shall be entitled to receive and shall receive from such state or the city, county, town or village thereof under which said position or employment was held by him, the same compensation therefor from the date of such unlawful removal to the date of his said restoration to said position or employment which he would have been entitled by law to have received in such position or employment but for such unlawful removal, and such veteran shall be entitled to a writ of mandamus to enforce the payment thereof, but such compensation or salary or wages, due in such position or employment, shall be subject to the provisions of sections 474 and 475 of the judiciary law for services rendered in either or both said special proceedings but otherwise shall be paid only directly to such veteran.

§ 24. Misdemeanor to obstruct right of examination; false representation; impersonation in examination.—Any commissioner, or examiner, or any other person who shall willfully by himself or in co-operation with other persons, defeat, deceive or obstruct any person in respect of his or her right of examination, or registration, according to any rules or regulations prescribed pursuant to the provisions of this chapter, or who shall willfully and falsely mark, grade, estimate or report upon the examination or proper standing of any person examined, registered or certified, pursuant to the provisions of this chapter, or aid in so doing, or who shall willfully make any false representations concerning the same, or concerning the person examined, or who shall willfully furnish to any person any special or secret information for the purpose of either improving or injuring the prospects or chances of any person so examined, registered or certified, or to be examined, registered or certified, or who shall personate any other person, or permit or aid in any manner any other person to personate him, in connection with any examination or registration, or application or request to be examined or registered, shall for each offense be deemed guilty of a misdemeanor.

§ 25. Recommendations for appointment or promotion.—No recommendation or question under the authority of this chapter shall relate to the political opinions or affiliations of any person whatever; and no appointment or selection to or removal from an office or employment within the scope of the rules established as aforesaid, shall be in any manner affected or influenced by such opinions or affiliations. No person in the civil service of the state or of any civil division or city thereof, is for that reason under any obligation to contribute to any political fund or to render any political service, and no person shall be removed or otherwise prejudiced for refusing so to do. No person in the said civil service shall discharge or promote or reduce, or in any manner change the official rank or compensation of any other person in said service, or promise or threaten so to do for giving or withholding or neglecting to make any contribution of money or service or any other valuable thing for any political purpose. No person in said service shall use his official authority or influence to coerce the political action of any person or body, or to interfere with any election.

§ 26. Political assessments prohibited.—No officer, agent, clerk or employee under the government of the state of New York or any civil division or city thereof shall, directly or indirectly, use his authority or official influence to compel or induce any other officer, clerk, agent or employee under said government, or any civil division or city thereof, to pay or promise to pay any political assessment, subscription or contribution. Every said officer, agent, clerk or employee who may have charge or control in any building, office or room occupied for any purpose of said government, or any said division or city thereof, is hereby authorized to prohibit the entry of any person, and he shall not knowingly permit any person to enter the same for the purpose of therein making, collecting, receiving or giving notice of any political assessment, subscription or contribution; and no person shall enter or remain in any said office, building or room, or send or direct any letter or other writing thereto, for the purpose of giving notice of, demanding or collecting a political assessment, nor shall any person therein give notice of, demand, collect or receive any such assessment, subscription or contribution; and no person shall prepare or make out, or take any part in preparing or making out, any political assessment, subscription or contribution with the intent that the same shall be sent or presented to or collected of any officer, agent or employee subject to the provisions of this chapter, under the government of the state of New York, or that of any civil division or city thereof, and no person shall knowingly send or present any political assessment, subscription or contribution to or request its payment of any said officer, agent or employee. Any person who shall be guilty of violating any provision of this section shall be deemed guilty of a misdemeanor.

§ 27. Officers or candidates not to promise influence, "public officer" and "public employee" defined.—Whoever, while holding any public office, or in nomination for, or while seeking a nomination or appointment for any public office, shall corruptly use or promise to use, whether directly or indirectly, any official authority or influence, whether then possessed or merely anticipated, in the way of conferring upon any person, or in order to secure or aid any person in securing any office or public employment, or any nomination, confirmation, promotion or increase of salary, upon the consideration or condition that the vote or political influence or action of the last-named person, or any other, shall be given or used in behalf of any candidate, officer, or party, or upon any other corrupt condition or consideration, shall be deemed guilty of bribery or an attempt at bribery. And whoever, being a public officer, or having or claiming to have any authority or influence for or affecting the nomination, public employment, confirmation, promotion, removal or increase or decrease of salary of any public officer, shall corruptly use, or promise, or threaten to use any such authority or influence, directly or indirectly, in order to coerce or persuade the vote or political action of any citizen or the removal, discharge or promotion of any officer or public employee, or upon any other corrupt consideration, shall also be guilty of bribery or of an attempt at bribery. Every person found guilty of such bribery, or an attempt to commit the same, as aforesaid, shall, upon conviction thereof, be liable to be punished by a fine of not less than one hundred dollars nor more than three thousand dollars, or to be imprisoned not less than ten days nor more than two years, or to both said fine and said imprisonment in the discretion of the court. The phrase "public officer" shall be held to include all public officials in this state, whether paid directly or indirectly from the public treasury of the state, or from that of any civil division thereof, or by fees or otherwise; and the phrase "public employee" shall be held to include every person not an officer who is paid from any said treasury.

§ 28. Taxpayer's action.—Any taxpayer shall have the right to bring an action in the supreme court to restrain the payment of salary or compensation to any person appointed to or holding any office, place or employment in violation of any of the provisions of this chapter, and such shall not be limited or denied by reason of the fact that said office, place or employment shall have been classified as, or determined to be, not subject to competitive examination; provided, however, that any judgment or injunction granted or made in any such action shall be prospective only, and shall not affect payments already made or due to such persons by the proper disbursing officers, in accordance with the civil service rules in force at the time of such payments.

ARTICLE III.

(Classification of state employees omitted.)

ARTICLE IV.

§ 60. Laws repealed.—Of the laws enumerated in the schedule hereto annexed, that portion specified in the last column is hereby repealed.

§ 61. When to take effect.—This chapter shall take effect immediately.

SCHEDULE OF LAWS REPEALED.

Laws of.	Chapter.	Sections.
1883	354	All.
1884	312	All.
1884	357	All.
1884	410	All.
1886	29	All.
1887	464	All.
1888	119	All.
1890	67	All.
1892	577	All.
1894	354	All.
1894	681	All.
1894	716	All.
1894	717	All.
1895	344	All.
1896	821	All.
1897	428	All.
1898	184	All.
1898	186	All.
1899	370	All.
1900	66	All.
1900	195	All.
1900	675	All.
1901	521	All.
1901	533	All.
1902	270	All.
1902	355	All.
1904	637	All.
1904	697	All.

CHARTER PROVISIONS

MUNICIPAL CIVIL SERVICE; MAYOR TO APPOINT COMMISSIONERS.

§ 123. The mayor shall appoint three or more suitable persons, not more than two-thirds of whom shall be members of the same political party, who shall, in the manner defined by chapter three of the general laws, commonly known as the civil service law, and subject to and in pursuance of the provisions of that law and of such amendments as may from time to time be made to it, prescribe, amend and enforce rules for the classification of the offices, places and employments in the public service of the city and for appointments and promotions therein, and examinations therefor, and for the registration and selection of laborers for employment therein. Such persons shall constitute the municipal civil service commission, and, within the amount appropriated therefor, they shall have authority to appoint a secretary, examiners, and such other subordinates as may be necessary. Proper provision shall be made in the annual budget for all the expenses of the municipal civil service commission.

REGULATIONS OF MUNICIPAL CIVIL SERVICE.

§ 124. All appointments, promotions and changes of status of persons in the public service of the city of New York shall be made in the manner prescribed by the constitution of the state and in accordance with the provisions of chapter three of the general laws, commonly known as the civil service law, and such amendments as may be made thereto, and the provisions of this act.

PROVISIONS OF THE CHARTER OF THE CITY OF NEW YORK.

Laws of 1901, Chapter 466.

AUTHORITY AND DUTY OF COMMISSIONERS OF MUNICIPAL CIVIL SERVICE.

§ 125. The municipal civil service commission shall have the power to make investigations concerning all matters touching the enforcement and effect of the provisions of the civil service law, in so far as it applies to The City of New York, and the rules and regulations prescribed thereunder, or concerning the action of any examiner or subordinate of the commission, or of any person in the classified municipal service, in respect to the execution of that act, and in the course of such investigations each commissioner and the secretary shall have the power to administer oaths. The municipal civil service commission shall have the further power to subpœna and require the attendance of witnesses, and the production thereby of books and papers pertinent to the investigations and inquiries hereby authorized, and to examine them, and such public records as it shall require in relation to any matter which it is required to investigate. For this purpose the commission shall possess all the powers conferred by the code of civil procedure upon a board or committee, and may invoke the power of any court of record in the state to compel the attendance and testifying of witnesses or the production thereby of books and papers as aforesaid.

Warrants for payment of salary of person whose appointment has not been made under civil service law, prohibited.

§ 126. Any officer of said city whose duty it is to sign or countersign warrants, shall not draw, sign or issue, or authorize the drawing, signing or issuing of any warrant on the chamberlain or other disbursing officer of the city for the payment of salary to any person in its service whose appointment or retention has not been in accordance with the civil service law and its amendments and of the valid rules in force thereunder.

Veterans in municipal service.

§ 127. All veterans either of the army or navy or the volunteer fire departments, now in the service of either of the municipal and public corporations hereby consolidated, who are now entitled by law to serve during good behavior, or who cannot under existing law be removed except for cause, shall be retained in like positions and under the same conditions by the corporation constituted by this act, to serve under such titles and in such way as the head of the appropriate department or the mayor may direct.

POLICE FORCE; QUALIFICATIONS OF MEMBERS; PUBLISHING NAMES AND RESIDENCE OF APPLICANTS AND APPOINTEES.

§ 284. No person shall be appointed or reappointed to membership in the police force or continue to hold membership therein, who is not a citizen of the United States or who has ever been convicted of felony, or who cannot read and write understandingly the English language, or who shall not have resided within the state, one year next preceding his appointment, but skilled officers of experience may be appointed for detective duty who have not resided as herein required. No person shall be appointed patrolman who shall be at the date of the filing of his application for civil service examination over twenty-nine years of age; no person shall be appointed doorman who shall be at the date of placing his name on the civil service eligible list over thirty-five years of age; and no person who shall have been a member of the force, and shall have been dismissed therefrom, shall be reappointed. The name, residence and occupation of each applicant for appointment or reappointment to any position in the police department, as well as the name, residence and occupation of each person appointed to any position, shall be published, and such publication shall, in every instance, be made, on the Saturday next succeeding such application, or appointment, in the City Record. Preliminary to a permanent appointment as patrolman there shall be a period of probation for such time as is fixed by the civil service rules, and no person shall receive a permanent appointment who has not served the required probationary period, but the service during probation shall be deemed to be service in the uniformed force, if succeeded by a permanent appointment, and as such shall be included and counted in determining eligibility for advancement, promotion, retirement and pension, as hereinafter provided. (As amended by L. 1912, ch. 480.)

Promotions in police force.

§ 288. Promotions of officers and members of the police force shall be made by the police commissioner, as provided in section one hundred and twenty-four of this act, on the basis of seniority, meritorious police service and a superior capacity, as shown by competitive examination, but no detail to act as inspector, or to service in the detective bureau, as hereafter provided, shall be deemed a promotion. Individual acts of personal bravery may be treated as an element of meritorious service in such examination, the relative rating therefor to be fixed by the municipal civil service commission. The police commissioner shall transmit to the municipal civil service commission in advance of such examination the complete record of each candidate for promotion. Sergeants shall be selected from among patrolmen of the first grade, but sergeants may be reduced to the grade of patrolman at any time by the police commissioner after due trial upon charges, the determination of which may be reviewed by writ of certiorari. Lieutenants of police shall be selected from among sergeants who shall have served at least two years continuously as such. Captains shall be selected from among lieutenants of police who shall have served at least three years as such. The police commissioner shall, in the exercise of his discretion, from time to time detail nineteen captains to act as inspectors, with the title while so acting of inspectors of police, and at his pleasure may revoke any or all such details. While so detailed such officer shall receive a salary at the rate of seven hundred and fifty dollars a year in addition to the amount of salary which regularly attaches to the office of captain. When a captain shall have acted under regular detail as inspector during a period or periods aggregating five years, such officer shall have the same rights in respect to the relief pension fund as were vested by law in inspectors of police on the first day of February in the year nineteen hundred and seven; provided, however, that when the commissioner designates a captain to act in the place of a captain under regular detail as inspector, during the temporary absence or disability of the latter, the officer so designated shall not be entitled to any additional salary, and the period of such designation shall not be counted in his favor in computing such five-year period. A captain, while detailed to act as inspector, shall be chargeable with and responsible for the discipline and efficiency of the force under his command. (As amended by L. 1907, ch. 160.)

Employment of engineers and architects.

§ 386. The president of each borough may at any time employ, when thereto authorized by the board of estimate and apportionment and the board of aldermen, a consulting engineer, who shall be an expert in all matters relating to sewers and highways, and who shall have had fifteen years' experience as a civil engineer; and a consulting engineer of public buildings, who shall be an expert in the matter of construction, repair and maintenance of public buildings; and a consulting architect, who shall be an architect of recognized, scientific and artistic standing of not less than fifteen years' experience. All other engineers or assistant engineers appointed by or under the authority of a borough president must be civil engineers of at least three years' experience. (As amended by L. 1906, ch. 565.)

DEPARTMENT OF STREET CLEANING; CHIEF ENGINEERS.

§ 453. The commissioner at the head of each of said departments, excepting the department of street cleaning, may appoint and at pleasure remove a chief engineer of his department, with power to appoint, remove and detail a staff of assistant engineers. If the commissioner of any department deem it advisable that more than one chief engineer be appointed for such department, such commissioner, when authorized by the board of estimate and apportionment and the board of aldermen, may appoint such additional chief engineers, each with power to appoint and remove at pleasure, and detail a staff of assistant engineers. All chief engineers appointed by them respectively, must be civil engineers of at least ten years' experience, and all assistant engineers appointed by them must be civil engineers of at least five years' experience. An engineer located at a branch office of his department in any borough may be appointed a deputy commissioner for the borough or boroughs to which he is assigned. An assistant engineer who has been appointed a deputy commissioner may be designated as the engineer for the borough in which he acts as deputy. Any engineer may be designated by such title as shall properly describe his principal duties in the judgment of the head of his department. (As amended by L. 1908, ch. 83.)

CONSULTING ENGINEERS.

§ 455. The commissioner of bridges may at any time employ, when thereto authorized by the board of estimate and apportionment and the board of aldermen, a consulting engineer, who shall be a recognized expert in bridge construction, and who shall have had not less than fifteen years' experience as a civil engineer. The commissioner of water supply, gas and electricity may at any time employ, when thereto authorized by the board of estimate and apportionment and the board of aldermen, a consulting hydraulic engineer to his department of at least fifteen years' experience as a civil engineer, and a consulting engineer of lighting and electricity to his department, who shall be an expert in all matters relating to lighting and electricity, and whose training shall also have included instruction in the capacity of civil engineer.

Sections 456–458, covering the duties of commissioners and heads of departments, and providing for the organization of bureaus therein, and chief engineer and deputy commissioner performing duties in more than one department, repealed by Amendatory Act of 1901, par. 2, infra.

TRANSFER OF EMPLOYEES FROM BOROUGH TO BOROUGH AND FROM DEPARTMENT TO DEPARTMENT.

§460. Nothing in this act contained shall be construed to limit in any way the power of the commissioner at the head of any one of the departments named in this chapter to transfer any employee or employees from the office of his department located in one borough to the office of his department in any other borough.

SELECTION OF SUBORDINATES.

§728. The fire commissioner shall have power to select heads of bureaus and assistants and as many officers and firemen as may be necessary, and they shall at all times be under the control of the fire commissioner, and shall perform such duties as may be assigned to them by him, under such names or titles as he may confer; provided, however, that assignments to duty and promotions in the uniformed force shall be made by the fire commissioner upon the recommendation of the chief of the department, and in case any recommendation so made by the chief shall be rejected, he shall within three days, submit another name or names and continue so to do until the assignment or promotion is made. Promotions of officers and members of the force shall be made by the fire commissioner as provided in section one hundred and twenty-four of this act on the basis of seniority, meritorious service in the department and superior capacity as shown by competitive examination. Individual acts of personal bravery may be treated as an element of meritorious service in such examination, the relative rating therefor to be fixed by the municipal civil service commission. The fire commissioner shall transmit to the municipal civil service commission in advance of such examination the complete record of each candidate for promotion.

QUALIFICATIONS OF FORCE OF FIRE DEPARTMENT.

§ 734. No person shall be appointed to membership in the fire department or continue to hold membership therein, who is not a citizen of the United States, or who has ever been convicted of felony; nor shall any person be appointed who cannot read and write understandingly the English language, or who shall not have resided within the state one year immediately prior to his appointment, or who is not over the age of twenty-one and at the date of the filing of his application for civil service examination was under the age of twenty-nine years. Every member of the uniformed force shall reside within the limits of the City of New York. Preliminary to a permanent appointment as fireman there shall be a period of probation for such time as is fixed by the civil service rules, and no person shall receive a permanent appointment who has not served the required probationary period, but the service during probation shall be deemed to be service in the uniformed force if succeeded by a permanent appointment, and as such shall be included and counted in determining eligibility for advancement, promotion, retirement and pension, as hereinafter provided. (As amended by L. 1912, ch. 462.)

APPORTIONMENT OF DEPUTY TAX COMMISSIONERS AMONG THE BOROUGHS.

§ 888. In making appointments of the deputy tax commissioners the head of the department of taxes and assessments shall apportion such appointments, as nearly as may be, among persons residing in the several boroughs created by this act, according to the population of the several boroughs; and, after the first day of January, 1902, no person shall be appointed to the office of deputy tax commissioner unless he shall be at the time he is appointed and shall have been at least one year prior thereto an elector in the borough from which he is appointed. No deputy tax commissioner shall be assigned to assess property in any other borough than that from which he is appointed, except by the vote of the board of taxes and assessments, and in that case the reasons for such a assignment shall be stated in the minutes of the board. (As amended by L. 1905, ch. 330.)

HEADS OF DEPARTMENTS; CONTROL OVER SUBORDINATES; REMOVAL.

§ 1543. The heads of all departments and all borough presidents (except as otherwise specially provided) shall have power to appoint and remove all chiefs of bureaus (except the chamberlain), as also all clerks, officers, employees and subordinates in their respective departments, except as herein otherwise specially provided, without reference to the tenure of office of any existing appointee. But no regular clerk or head of a bureau, or person holding a position in the classified municipal civil service subject to competitive examination, shall be removed until he has been allowed an opportunity of making an explanation; and in every case of a removal, the true grounds thereof shall be forthwith entered upon the records of the department or board or borough president, and a copy filed with the municipal civil service. In case of removal, a statement showing the reason therefor shall be filed in the department. The number of all officers, clerks, employees, laborers and subordinates in every department shall be such as the heads of the respective departments and borough presidents shall designate and approve, not exceeding the number limited by any ordinance of the board of aldermen. The duties of all such officers, clerks, employees, laborers and subordinates shall be such as the heads of the respective departments and borough presidents shall designate and approve, subject to the provisions of law and to the ordinances of the board of aldermen. The salaries or wages of all such officers, clerks, employees, laborers and subordinates in every department shall be such as shall be fixed by the board of aldermen upon the recommendation of the board of estimate and apportionment in the manner provided in this act. Any head of department or borough president, may, with the consent of the board of estimate and apportionment, consolidate any two or more bureaus established by law, and may change the duties of any bureau; and it shall be the duty of the head of the finance department to bring together all officers and bureaus authorized to receive money for taxes, assessments or arrears, in such manner that the payment of the same can be made, as nearly as practicable, at one time and place, and in one office. Every head of department or borough president, and every officer of any of the counties contained within the territorial limits of The City of New York, is empowered to make ratable deductions from the salaries and wages of the employees and subordinates of his department or office on account of absence from duty without leave; provided, however, that nothing contained in this section shall affect departments or offices as to which other provision is made by this act for deductions for absence or disciplinary fines and penalties. Wherever in any department or institution an office, position or employment is abolished, or made unnecessary through the operation of this act, or in any other manner, or whenever the number of offices, positions or employments of a certain character is reduced, the person or persons legally holding the office or filling the position or employment thus abolished or made unnecessary shall be deemed to be suspended without pay, and shall be entitled to reinstatement in the same office, position or employment, or in any corresponding or similar office, position or employment, if within one year thereafter there is need for his or their services. Whenever such offices, positions or employments are abolished or made unnecessary, it shall be the duty of the head of the department or institution to furnish the names of the person or persons affected to the municipal civil service commission, with a statement in the case of each of the date of his original appointment in the service. It shall be the duty of the municipal civil service commission forthwith to place the names of said persons upon a list of suspended employees for the office, or position or for the class of work in which they have been employed, or for any corresponding or similar office, position or class of work, and to certify the said persons for reinstatement, in the order of their original appointment, before making certifications from any other list. The failure of any person on any such list for reinstatement to accept, after reasonable notice, an office or position in the same borough and at the same salary or wages as the position formerly held by him shall be held to be a relinquishment of his right to reinstatement as herein stated.

Laws of 1907, Chapter 723.

POLICE AND FIRE COMMISSIONERS MAY REHEAR CHARGES AND REINSTATE MEMBERS OF FORCE.

§ 1543-a. Upon written application to the mayor by the person aggrieved, setting forth the reasons for demanding such rehearing, the police commissioner, if the person aggrieved was a member of the police force, or the fire commissioner, if the person aggrieved was a member of the fire department, shall have the power, in his discretion, to rehear the charges upon which a member of the uniformed police or fire department, as the case may be, has been dismissed, unless such dismissal was for insubordination, conduct unbecoming an officer or member, cowardice or intoxication; provided that such former member of such force or department shall waive in writing all claim against The City of New York for back pay and provided further that the mayor shall, in writing, consent to such rehearing, stating the reasons why such charges should be reheard.

Such application for a rehearing shall be made within one year after this act takes effect or within one year from the date of the removal if such removal occurs after this act takes effect.

If such commissioner shall determine that such member has been illegally or unjustly dismissed, such commissioner may reinstate such member and allow him the whole of his time since such dismissal, to be applied on his time of service in such department, or for such other or further relief as such commissioner may determine just, or to affirm his dismissal as he may determine from the evidence.

Laws of 1913, Chapter 302.

HEADS OF DEPARTMENTS OTHER THAN THE POLICE AND FIRE COMMISSIONER MAY REHEAR CHARGES AGAINST AND REINSTATE PERSONS DISMISSED.

§ 1543-b. The head of a city department or any other officer board or body of the city, or of a borough, or of a county, vested with the power of appointment and employment, except the police commissioner and the fire commissioner, upon written application by the person aggrieved, setting forth the reasons for demanding an opportunity of making a further explanation, shall have the power, in his discretion, to rehear the explanation and any new matter offered in further reply to the charges or complaint upon which such person was dismissed from the service, provided that such person shall waive, in writing, all claim against the city of New York for back pay. Such application for another opportunity to explain shall only be presented to, and granted by the officer who made the removal or to the immediate successor of the removing official when the applicant for the further explanation makes it appear, by affidavit, that on a further chance to explain he can produce evidence such as if before received would probably have changed the decision; if such evidence has been discovered since the previous explanation; is not cumulative; and the failure to produce it at the first explanation was not owing to want to diligence. No reinstatement by a successor shall be made where the applicant has been removed more than two years, nor without the consent of the mayor. If upon further explanation such head of department or other officer, board or body determine that such person has been illegally or unjustly dismissed, such head of department or other officer, board or body, in his discretion, may, upon the approval in writing of the municipal civil service commission, reinstate such persons.

City employees; vacations regulated.

§ 1567. The executive heads of the various departments are authorized and empowered to grant to every employee of the city of New York, or of any department or bureau thereof, and of the department of education, a vacation of not less than two weeks in each year and for such further period of time as the duties, length of service and other qualifications of an employee may warrant, at such time as the executive head of the department or any officer having supervision over said employee may fix, and for such time they shall be allowed the same compensation as if actually employed, except that no such vacation shall be granted to per diem employees for more than one week, and only during the months of June, July and August.

(Added by L. 1909, ch. 559.)

Per diem employees; leave of absence with pay.

§ 1568. The head of a city department, or any other officer, board or body of the city, or of a borough or county within the city, vested with the power of appointment and employment, in addition to existing powers, may, in his discretion, grant to an employee in his department, board, body or office, whose compensation is payable by the day and who may be injured in the performance of his duties, a leave of absence during disability with pay, which leave of absence, however, shall not exceed thirty days except with the consent of the mayor and the comptroller. (L. 1912, Ch. 353.)

OFFICERS AND EMPLOYEES; PUNISHMENT FOR DELINQUENCY OR MISCONDUCT.

§ 1569. Except as otherwise specially provided, the head of a city department or any other officer, board or body of the city, or of a borough or county within the city, vested with the power of appointment and employment, in addition to existing powers, may, in his discretion, cause deductions to be made from the salaries, compensation or wages of the officers or employees of his department, board, body or office, as a fine for delinquency or misconduct, not exceeding thirty days' pay. (L. 1912, ch. 432.)

OFFICERS AND EMPLOYEES; LEAVE OF ABSENCE WITHOUT PAY.

§ 1569-*b*. Except as otherwise specially provided, the head of a city department or any other officer, board or body of the city, or of a borough or county within the city, vested with the power of appointment and employment, in addition to existing powers, may, in his discretion, upon application of any officer or employee of such department, office, board or body, grant to such officer or employee a leave of absence from duty without pay. (L. 1912, ch. 251.)

ORDINANCES OF THE CITY OF NEW YORK.

AN ORDINANCE to prevent non-residents of the State of New York from holding employment in any of the departments or branches of the government of The City of New York.

BE IT ORDAINED, by the Board of Aldermen of
The City of New York, as follows:

§ 1. No person not a citizen and an actual resident and dweller in good faith in, the State of New York shall be eligible to appointment or employment in any of the departments, boards, bureaus or branches of the government of The City of New York.

§ 2. Any person who now is, or who shall become after such appointment or employment, a citizen, resident or dweller outside the State of New York, shall thereby forfeit and shall be removed from his said appointment or employment.

§ 3. The provisions of this ordinance shall not apply to appointments or employments for services or work to be performed for The City of New York outside the State of New York; nor to a temporary appointment or employment for a specified service or work where peculiar or exceptional qualifications of a scientific, professional or educational character are necessary. Prior to such temporary appointment or employment evidence in writing shall be furnished that the services or work to be performed cannot be well done by any citizen and actual resident of the State of New York who can be discovered, and that the non-resident person proposed to be appointed or employed is generally recognized as one possessing such exceptional qualifications in a high degree. No appointment or employment under this section shall be valid unless the consent of the Mayor shall be first obtained; and he may require the Civil Service Commission to pass upon the matter, and certify whether such appointment or employment is necessary, and whether the non-resident person proposed therefor be competent, and also necessary for lack of a citizen and actual resident of the State of New York who is competent.

§ 4. This ordinance shall take effect October first, nineteen hundred and thirteen.

Adopted by the Board of Aldermen, April 29, 1913.

GENERAL REGULATIONS OF THE COMMISSION

MUNICIPAL CIVIL SERVICE COMMISSION

GENERAL REGULATIONS

Regulation I.

THE SECRETARY.

1. The Secretary shall keep the minutes of the proceedings of the Commission, and shall keep records of all appointments, promotions, transfers, reinstatements, removals or other changes of status under these rules or other action thereunder. He shall have charge of all books, eligible lists, records and papers, and of the official seal and other property in the Commission's office.

2. He shall keep the official roster and have charge of the certification of all payrolls and estimates submitted in pursuance of Rule XXI.

3. He shall prepare from time to time, for submission to the Commission, blank forms covering, so far as practicable, all applications, certificates, reports, records and returns required in connection with the work of his office.

4. Unless otherwise ordered, he shall, under the direction of the President and after consultation with the Chief Examiner, set the dates for examinations and make all requisite public announcement of such examinations and other proposed changes.

5. He shall notify all candidates for examination, whose applications have been accepted, of the time and place fixed for such examination, and of the conditions thereof.

6. He shall make all certifications to appointing officers, upon their requisition, of candidates eligible to appointment, promotion or employment.

7. He shall, subject to the direction of the Commission, assign and direct the work of all subordinate employees except those subordinate to the Chief Examiner.

8. He shall audit and certify the accounts of the salaries and expenses of the Commission and of all its subordinates, conduct the official correspondence, and perform such other appropriate duties as the Commission may assign to him.

9. The Assistant Secretary shall act under the direction of the Secretary, as his assistant, and shall perform the duties of the Secretary in his absence.

Regulation II.

THE CHIEF EXAMINER.

The Chief Examiner, subject to the direction of the Commission, shall have charge of all matters pertaining to the preparation for, and conduct of examinations, except as herein otherwise provided. He shall:

1. Prepare, for submission to the Commission, blank forms covering, so far as practicable, the details of the work of his office.

2. Determine, in the first instance, all questions relating to the eligibility of candidates for examinations based upon their written application, except such as relate to particulars appearing on the face thereof, and also questions relating to the admissibility of candidates when they appear for examination.

3. Prepare and communicate to the Secretary forms for all advertisements of competitive examinations required under Rule VII and of all schedules of examinations, and announcements of the conditions thereof, required to be published at the beginning of each year.

4. Direct the work of examiners or other employees subordinate to him, and take care to secure accuracy, uniformity and justice in their proceedings.

5. Designate a person to enter a detailed account of each examination in a book, which shall form part of the records of the Commission. This account shall be entered as soon as practicable

after an examination and shall be dated and signed by the person making the entries. It shall show the date and place of examination; the position for which it was held; the conditions governing the examination and all details connected therewith.

6. There shall be entered an account of all dismissals and withdrawals from the examination, which shall state the preliminary number of the candidate and the subject upon which he was working at the time of dismissal or withdrawal. In the case of dismissals, the exact cause therefor, the time and the action taken thereon by the Chief Examiner or other person in charge of the examination, shall be stated. In the case of withdrawals, the reason for such withdrawal shall be stated, if this be given by the candidate. The time of such withdrawal shall also be stated, if it is believed that such information may afterwards be useful to the Commission.

7. Whenever practicable, all notes of examiners and monitors regarding the details of the examination shall be made on the day of the examination and the time of each incident shall be given.

8. Audit all accounts for compensation of examiners and monitors employed at a per diem rate, and for all other expenses arising in the Examining Department.

9. Perform such other appropriate duties as may be specified in the rules or in these regulations or assigned to him by the Commission.

Regulation III.

ASSISTANT CHIEF EXAMINERS.

The duties of the Assistant Chief Examiners shall be to prepare questions in examinations, to rate candidates' papers and to perform such other appropriate duties as may be assigned to them by the Commission.

An Assistant Chief Examiner to be designated by the Commission shall, subject to the provisions of Rule VII, have general supervision over the work of the examiners engaged in rating the papers in open competitive examinations and non-competitive examinations.

An Assistant Chief Examiner to be designated by the Commission shall, subject to the provisions of Rule VII, have charge of promotion examinations and shall perform such duties relative thereto as may be assigned to him by the Commission. He shall have general supervision of the work of the examiners engaged in the rating of papers in promotion examinations.

An Assistant Chief Examiner to be designated by the Commission shall administer the office and perform the duties of the Chief Examiner when he is absent from the office.

Regulation IV.

THE CHIEF CLERK.

The Chief Clerk shall be subject to the direction of the Secretary and shall have charge of all matters relating to and affecting the administration of the Application Bureau, Certification Bureau, Payroll Bureau and Record Room.

Regulation V.

The Secretary, the Chief Examiner and the Chief Clerk shall take care that the rules and regulations are complied with, and shall bring to the attention of the Commission all instances within their respective offices in which it appears that any provision thereof has been violated or disregarded by any public officer or employee, or by any other person.

Regulation VI.

APPLICATION.

1. Applicants for positions in the Competitive or the Labor Class shall specify in each case the position or positions for which they wish to apply.

2. No application will be accepted from any person:

(*a*) Who is not a citizen of the United States, except that this requirement may be waived by the resolution of the Commission in the case of positions requiring scientific, educational or professional qualifications of a high or unusual order;

(*b*) Who is not a resident of the state, or of the city, or of a particular borough, where such residence is required by law;

(*c*) Who is physically disqualified for or who is not within the age limits fixed for the positions sought;

(*d*) Who is addicted to the excessive use of intoxicating beverages or drugs;

(*e*) Who, within two years preceding the date of application, has been dismissed from any position in the city service for delinquency or misconduct; unless otherwise ordered by the Commission;

(*f*) Who, within nine months, has failed in or withdrawn from an examination for the same position, unless this requirement be waived by resolution of the Commission in accordance with clause 12 of Rule VII.;

(*g*) Who has knowingly made a false statement in his application, or who has been guilty of fraud or deceit in connection therewith; or

(*h*) Who is otherwise ineligible under any of the provisions of the Civil Service Law or Rules.

3. If the applicant claims rights of preference as a veteran, he must prove his claim by presenting for record (1) his original discharge, (2) certificate from the Adjutant-General or Records and Pension Bureau of the War Department or Secretary of the Navy; or (3) certificate from Adjutant-General of the State in which he served. If he served under other than his proper name, affidavits from two of his former company must accompany his discharge (or certificate) unless he is receiving a pension, in which case his pension certificate will be sufficient proof of identity. If the slightest doubt exists as to identity, service or residence of the applicant, he may be required to produce further proof in support of his claim.

4. All applications presented for positions in the Competitive Class shall be indexed under the Card System, and, before acceptance, shall be verified as to the applicant's eligibility for the examination sought.

5. Applications for examination for positions in the Non-competitive Class shall be addressed to the officer having the power of appointment to such positions, and shall not be received by the Commission.

Regulation VII.

AGE LIMITATIONS.

1. The limits of age at the time of application for the following-named positions in the Competitive Class shall be as follows:

Position	Minimum	Maximum
Fireman	21	29
Patrolman	21	29
Prison Keeper	21	35
Police Matron	30	40
Clerk, 1st grade	..	18
Clerk, 2d grade	17	25
Stenographer and Typewriter	18	..
Axeman	18	..
Junior Draughtsman	18	..
And for all other positions, unless otherwise prescribed	21	..

2. The limits of age at the time of application for the following named positions in the Labor Class shall be as follows:

Position	Minimum	Maximum
Driver, Department of Street Cleaning	21	40
Dumpboardman, Department of Street Cleaning	21	40
Hostler, Department of Street Cleaning	21	40
Scowman, Department of Street Cleaning	21	40
Stableman, Department of Street Cleaning	21	40
Sweeper, Department of Street Cleaning	21	40
Batteryman's Assistant	18	..
Blacksmith' Helper	18	..
Boilermaker's Helper	18	..
Electrician's Helper	18	..
Machinist's Helper	18	..
Plumber's Helper	18	..
Steamfitter's Helper	18	..
For all other positions	21	..

Regulation VIII.

PHYSICAL QUALIFICATIONS.

Candidates for the following positions in the Competitive Class will be required to pass a medical examination, testing their capacity physically for the discharge of the duties peculiar to the position sought, before admission to the competitive examination:

Positions in any grade of the Police, Fire, Street Cleaning or Prison services, whether filled by appointment or promotion; Police Matron, Matron, Nurse, Attendant, Court Attendant, Messenger, Watchman, Bridge Keeper, Janitor, Janitor Engineer, Prison Orderly, Orderly, and such other positions as the Commission may from time to time, designate.

Regulation IX.

QUALIFICATIONS FOR SPECIAL POSITIONS.

1. Candidates for professional positions of any character will be required to present, among the preliminary evidences of their fitness, the certificates, diplomas, or licenses required by law for the practice of their respective professions in the State of New York.

2. For positions requiring the practice of chemistry, candidates must present proof that they have received the degree of Bachelor of Science, or its equivalent, or present a certificate from some reputable institution showing that they have pursued for two years a course of study therein tending to qualify them for the position sought.

3. Candidates for the position of Inspector in the Bureaus of Buildings must show before appointment that they have had at least five years' practical experience as an architect, engineer, mason, carpenter or plumber, or, if the application be for the position of Chief Inspector of Buildings, that they have had at least ten years' practical experience as an architect, engineer or builder.

4. Candidates for the position of Assistant Engineer in any bureau subject to a Borough President must be civil engineers of at least three years' experience (chapter 386 of the Greater New York Charter). Candidates for the position of Assistant Engineer in the Department of Water Supply, Gas and Electricity, the Department of Bridges, or the Department of Street Cleaning, must

be civil engineers of at least five years' experience (chapter 453 of the Greater New York Charter).

5. Candidates for the position of Court Clerk, Stenographer or Attendant in the City Magistrates' Court, or in the Municipal Court, must be residents of the borough or other prescribed geographical division in which the court in which they are to be appointed is situated.

6. Candidates for the position of Deputy Tax Commissioner must show before appointment that, for at least one year prior thereto, they have been electors in the borough in which they are to serve.

7. Candidates for the positions of Stationary Engineer and Janitor Engineer must produce, in advance of the examination, either an engineer's license or the affidavits of three licensed engineers certifying, in each case, to the candidate's qualification for the duties of the position.

Regulation X.

EXAMINATIONS.

1. Applicants must present themselves promptly at the examination rooms at the hour and place specified in the notification from the Secretary's office, and none will be admitted to an examination except upon the production of such notification.

2. Applicants, if required, must provide themselves with the pens, penholders, erasers, ink and blotters they are to use, but they shall not use in the examination room any writing paper but that furnished by the Commission or notes of any description.

Applicants for an examination for stenography and typewriting shall provide themselves with typewriting machines and appurtenances. Those to be examined for the position of draughtsman, or for any other position requiring the use of instruments, must furnish the instruments.

3. Before the commencement of the examination the weight to be given to each subject included therein, the minimum percentage necessary to secure a passing mark and the time allowed for the completion of the examination shall be announced to the competitors orally or in a printed or written memorandum. No questions given

to a competitor at any session of an examination may be answered at another session.

4. The name of the candidate must not be written on any of his examination papers, and specific announcement shall be made by a memorandum printed on each examination sheet that any paper bearing the name of the competitor, or any other identifying mark, will be rejected.

5. The following instructions shall be furnished to each competitor, in printed form, before the examination papers are distributed, and both competitors and examiners shall be bound thereby:

1. Candidates shall read carefully the printed instructions before beginning work. They will be bound by the following rules, as well as by the instructions given to each competitor at the beginning of an examination.

2. They must put their preliminary numbers on the notices to appear, fill out the preliminary sheet, including all blanks, sign their names thereon and inclose the preliminary sheet and notice in the envelope provided and seal the envelope and hand it to the examiner.

3. Each paper written by a candidate shall be marked with his or her examination number, but if the candidate's name or any other identifying mark is used the paper will not be rated.

4. Candidates must observe that each question sheet is received in proper order, and be sure that none of the sheets have been omitted. They are held responsible for all errors and omissions.

5. Candidates must not leave their desks with a sheet unfinished unless required to do so by nature of the examination. A candidate who leaves the room while engaged on a paper will not be allowed to finish that paper.

6. They are allowed to leave the examination room for luncheon at such time as may be announced at the examination. No additional time will be allowed on account of absence.

7. All necessary additional sheets of examination paper upon which to complete work may be had upon application to an examiner or monitor. Answers should not be written on the question sheets, but on the ruled sheets provided for that purpose.

8. In writing, pencil work will not be allowed, but in an examination where drawing is a test, sketches may be made in pencil.

9. Pencil and scratch paper may be used for preliminary work except for spelling, which must be written with ink directly on the ruled sheets from the dictation of the examiner.

10. No scratch paper may be used except that furnished by the examiner in charge, and on finishing the answers all the scratch paper should be destroyed by the candidate and must not be taken from the room.

11. No help is allowed except what appears on the question sheet or in the instructions given candidates.

12. Candidates who may be detected in consulting any printed or written matter during an examination will be dismissed.

13. All conversation or communication between candidates during examination is strictly forbidden. Speaking to a neighbor on any pretense or replying to him if he speaks, will result in dismissal from the examination room.

14. It is forbidden to copy or to attempt to read from the work of any competitor, or to permit any competitor to copy from or to read the sheets of another. It is absolutely forbidden to make any signs or in any manner to seek to impart or to receive any information of any kind or description during an examination, under penalty of dismissal.

15. All necessary explanations will be made when practicable to the whole number of competitors.

16. All examination papers must be handed in with the answers and must not be taken from the room.

Regulation XI.

SUBJECTS AND WEIGHTS.

1. The subjects of an examination, with the weights attaching thereto, shall be announced by the examiner in charge at time and place of examination.

2. Except where otherwise specifically provided by either the rules or these regulations, questions in examination for original

appointment shall relate to the general fitness and capacity of the candidates rather than to their knowledge of the rules or methods of the department or departments in which the positions they are seeking exist

Regulation XII.

MARKING AND GRADING.

1. The examiners assigned for the making of papers shall complete such marking as soon as practicable after the completion of an examination. Such marking shall be under the direction of the Chief Examiner.

2. The marking of the papers of each competitor shall be made on the scale of 100, which shall represent the maximum possible attainment. The average of the marking of the several answers upon any one subject shall be the standing on that subject.

3. The general average standing of each competitor shall be made up in accordance with the weights attaching respectively to the several subjects substantially as follows:

SUBJECTS	Standing on Subject	Weight Given to Subject	Product of Standing and Weight
1. Handwriting	83	30	2,490
2. Writing from dictation	90	15	1,350
3. English spelling	68	15	1,020
4. Arithmetic	72	20	1,440
5. Making summary	70	20	1,400
Total product	..	..	7,700
Divide product by sum of weights	..	100	
General average standing	..	..	77
6. Letter writing	..	..	85

As indicated, the standing on each subject shall be multiplied by the weight given such subject and the product placed in the third column, and the sum of these products divided by the sum of the weights will give the general average.

4. Where the weight attaching to any subject in any examination is not less than six out of ten, and candidates are required to obtain a general average percentage of 70 in such examination, the papers so weighted shall be rated first, and the papers of a candidate who fails to receive a mark of at least 50 thereon shall not be rated further. Where any examination includes a technical subject for which a rating of 75 is required, the papers relating to such subject shall be rated first, and the papers of a candidate who fails to receive a mark of at least 72 thereon shall not be rated, but this plan may not be adhered to where, in the opinion of the Chief Examiner, the work of marking is not facilitated thereby. The schedule sheet shall show the ratings on each subject of all candidates who receive a percentage of at least 50 on a paper bearing a weight of six out of ten, or of at least 72 on a technical paper, but in the case of candidates failing to receive such required averages shall contain the ratings received on such papers only.

5. In any appeal from the markings of the examiners, the candidates must refer to the particular paper which, for such reasons as he may state, he believes was not fairly marked.

6. Where an appeal is made, action upon which would involve a change of any rating, such appeal before such action is taken shall be referred for report to the Chief Examiner and the examiners by whom the original markings were made.

7. Where an appeal has reference to any medical examination or test, it must be accompanied by a physician's certificate with reference to the facts upon which it is based.

Regulation XIII.

ELIGIBLE LISTS.

1. The Chief Examiner shall report to the Secretary the results of each examination, giving the names and ascertained average markings of all competitors who completed such examination, and the names of all who withdrew therefrom, together with such other information with reference thereto as may be necessary for the information of the Commission. The Secretary shall thereupon

enter upon the appropriate eligible lists, in the manner required by Rule X., the names of all persons who have received the required minimum percentage.

2. Within five days after the establishment of a list, each candidate whose name appears thereon shall be advised by the Secretary by mail as to the percentage he has secured and his relative position on the list, and the Secretary shall inform such candidate as to changes in his relative position on the list due to the making of appointments therefrom or to other causes, whenever a request for such information is made.

3. Each eligible list shall be published, as soon as practicable after it is established, in the "City Record." The lists shall be open to public inspection, but copies thereof shall be furnished to no one except to appointing officers having the right of selection therefrom, or except in accordance with section 1545 of the Charter. The names of persons who have received less than the minimum standing shall not be published under any circumstances.

Regulation XIV.

CERTIFICATION AND APPOINTMENT.

1. The Secretary shall make certification of eligibles upon the requisition of appointing officers in such form as the Commission shall prescribe. No appointments shall be made from any certification after the expiration of the term of the eligible list from which such certification is made.

2. Where certification is required to be made according to residence, the residence of any candidate shall be deemed to be the place stated by him in his application to be his legal residence, at the time such application was filed; but in case the candidate has removed from the borough or other prescribed geographical division in which he resided at the time of his application, he shall no longer be eligible to appointment.

3. On the request of an appointing officer, the Commission shall submit to his inspection at its office, the application and examination papers of any candidate certified for appointment, or shall furnish him in connection with such certification, with the

names of the certifiers and of the employers during the five years immediately preceding the application of each such candidate, to permit the addressing of such inquiries to such certifiers or employers as such officer may wish to make.

4. When the name of an eligible is certified for appointment or employment, a notice shall be given him to that effect, specifying the department to which the certification has been made, the title of the position and the compensation offered.

5. When the name of an eligible is certified for appointment and such eligible has declined appointment by reason of temporary inability, such declination shall not continue in effect for a longer period than three months from the date of certification.

Regulation XV.

THE LABOR CLASS.

1. Applications for employment in the Labor Class shall be received only for positions the titles of which are classified.

2. Each applicant shall be given a receipt for his application, on which shall be noted his name, address, the position sought, the date and the application number, and such number shall be furnished to the applicant on his request at any future time.

3. Applicants must report for the physical examination promptly at the time and place stated in the notice given thereof, and must present the notice of examination before they can be examined.

4. The results of the physical examination shall be entered on the application form of the applicant, and following the examination both the said form and notice of examination shall be stamped with the date and the word "Examined." Should the applicant fail to pass, the form shall be stamped with the word "Rejected." The notice shall be returned to the applicant. The following are causes of rejection for all titles in the Labor Class:

Defect of any extremity necessitating artificial aid or support.

Tuberculosis of all kinds.

Hernia, inguinal or scrotal.

Vision below 20-30.

Hearing, markedly impaired (except in the case of boilermakers and some other workers in allied trades, who, from the nature of the work are more or less subject to aural defects).

Obesity.

Inability to fully extend above the head a dumbbell with each arm.

Evidence of Syphilis and excessive use of alcohol or drugs.

5. Certification of eligibles for employment as laborers shall be made in the manner prescribed for positions in the competitive class, and the appointing officer, or his representative, shall forward to the Commission an identification sheet with such entries as may be necessary to permit of their comparison with the statements and description of the applicant at the time of his application for registration.

6. The minimum relative measurements required for the position of Driver, Department of Street Cleaning, shall be as follows:

Height	*Weight*	*Height*	*Weight*
5 feet 4 inches	130 pounds	5 feet 9 inches	155 pounds
5 " 5 "	135 "	5 " 10 "	160 "
5 " 6 "	140 "	5 " 11 "	165 "
5 " 7 "	145 "	6 " and over	170 "
5 " 8 "	150 "		

INDEX TO THE RULES OF THE CIVIL SERVICE COMMISSION

INDEX TO CIVIL SERVICE LAW.

INDEX TO CHARTER PROVISIONS.

INDEX TO REGULATIONS.

www.ingramcontent.com/pod-product-compliance
Lightning Source LLC
LaVergne TN
LVHW021406110826
845150LV00007B/1802

9781425511890